ORDINARY EQUALITY

ORDINARY EQUALITY

THE FEARLESS WOMEN AND QUEER PEOPLE WHO SHAPED THE U.S. CONSTITUTION AND THE EQUAL RIGHTS AMENDMENT

KATE KELLY

ART BY NICOLE LARUE

GIBBS SMITH
TO ENRICH AND INSPIRE HUMANKIND

First Edition
26 25 24 23 22 5 4 3 2

Published by Gibbs Smith
P.O. Box 667 Layton, Utah 84041
1.800.835.4993 orders
www.gibbs-smith.com

Art and design by Nicole LaRue, Small Made Goods 2022
Cover art based on photo by Patrick Poend/Shutterstock.com
Printed and bound in China

Gibbs Smith books are printed on either recycled,
100% post-consumer waste, FSC-certified papers or on paper produced
from sustainable PEFC-certified forest/controlled wood source.
Learn more at www.pefc.org.

Library of Congress Cataloging-in-Publication Data:

Names: Kelly, Kathleen, 1980– author.
Title: Ordinary Equality: the Fearless Women and Queer People Who Shaped the U.S.
Constitution and the Equal Rights Amendment / Kate Kelly.
Description: First edition. | Layton, Utah: Gibbs Smith, [2022] | Includes bibliographical references.
Identifiers: LCCN 2021025788 | ISBN 9781423658726 (hardcover) | ISBN 9781423658733 (epub)
Subjects: LCSH: Women—United States—Biography. | Political Activists—United States—Biography. |
Feminists—United States—Biography. | Women's rights. | LCGFT: Biographies.
Classification: LCC HQ1412 .K45 2020 | DDC 920.72—dc23 LC record available at
https://lccn.loc.gov/2021025788

To Jim Kelly and all the other dads who—
instead of grounding their daughters—
build them a launchpad and provide a steady supply of rocket fuel

CONTENTS

A NOTE FROM THE AUTHOR

While referring to women formally and using their proper
titles is an important way to respect them, in this book I have
chosen to refer to them by their first names in the hope of making them familiar to us. I want them to feel like the complex,
relatable people they were and are—not distant, unreachable
figures from ancient history. In addition, referring to them
by their surnames did not make sense for *Ordinary Equality*
because that would mean (thanks to the patriarchy) many would
solely be referred to by either their husband's or father's names.
Referring to them by their first names is a way to
reclaim what is authentically theirs.

HISTORY TENDS TO BURY WHAT IT SEEKS TO REJECT, AND IT WAS NO ACCIDENT THAT MALE-DOMINATED HISTORY EXCISED THE LEADERSHIP OF WOMEN.

BLANCHE WIESEN COOK,
Crystal Eastman on Women and Revolution

INTRODUCTION
CENTERING WOMEN IN HISTORY

I SAT OPPOSITE US SENATOR Orrin Hatch's legislative aide. He was wearing an ill-fitting suit and had a notepad in front of him. The notepad was a conduit for the soft but steady tapping of his pen, a metronome broadcasting his impatience. Helene de Boissiere-Swanson, founder of Katrina's Dream—an organization she started to pursue her mother-in-law, Katrina's, wish for the full inclusion of women in the church and society—was sitting across from me at the conference table. She had just given the aide a long soliloquy about constitutional equality and was now bent down, rummaging through the large trekking backpack she had brought with her into the office. Without warning, she slammed a clear plastic container with a red lid onto the table. It was filled with a gray powdery substance.

"Women have been waiting nearly one hundred years, and in the name of my dead husband, who is here with us today"— Helene said as she dramatically gestured toward the container, which I slowly realized was filled with human remains—"we must ratify the Equal Rights Amendment!" The poor legislative aide blinked incredulously, speechless. My jaw dropped. What could there possibly be left to say after that? We abruptly ended the meeting and shuffled out.

Once we were safely in the lobby of the Federal Building in Salt Lake City, our hearty little band of local ERA advocates regrouped. Inexplicably, Helene seemed pleased and explained that this had been one of her more productive meetings. Having been on a months-long solo "pilgrimage" across the country in support of ERA ratification, she walked America's highways and byways, stopping at each tiny tavern and Podunk church along the way with her bright green circular ERA YES sign, sharing the gospel of equality with every single person she encountered. As part of a group trying to revive the organization Mormons for ERA, a few of us had agreed to join Helene at Senator Hatch's office sight unseen. We'd never been granted a meeting with any elected officials before, and thanks to her unorthodox approach, I realized tenacity was the secret weapon.

SLC Federal Building

SO HOW DID WE as a country end up without women's rights in our Constitution, and the Equal Rights Amendment still not integrated *one hundred years* after it was first written? And how did I end up in that room with Helene and her container of ashes? My personal story has a lot to do with the path of the ERA and a woman named Sonia Johnson, one of the many audacious women throughout history who has fought to change our constitution and ratify the ERA.

I was raised Mormon. Mormonism, like most religions, teaches that there are good people and there are bad people. The good people are pious Mormons who adhere to very strict doctrine, including traditional gender roles. The bad people stray from those hard-set rules. My initial introduction to the ERA came from learning about one of those "bad people"—Sonia Johnson. She had been excommunicated from my church in the 1980s. At the time, this thought was horrifying to me. Why would someone stray so far and risk being ostracized from the community—forever! Well, it turns out she was hell-bent on was equal rights for women.

The Equal Rights Amendment was introduced in every Congress since 1923 and finally passed in 1972. Then it went to the states for ratification. (The Constitution requires three-quarters of the states ratify an amendment.) My mom and grandma fought in the ERA battle in the 1970s, but on the opposite side of Sonia Johnson. My grandma had been assigned by the church to speak out against ERA ratification in her home state of Arizona. Once, as I was flipping through one of my mom's old scrapbooks, I found an article she had written opposing the ERA in her college newspaper *The Daily Wildcat*. It was so odd to read her arguing *against* equality. If good, intelligent women like my mom and grandma had been so passionately against the ERA, why had Sonia been for it?

In the late seventies, it was a race against the clock to get the final three states to ratify the ERA, and Mormons and other conservative groups were fighting hard to kill it. The Mormon prophet and his two counselors wrote an official statement against the ERA in 1976 and repeated it in 1978 in "Reaffirmation of the First Presidency's Position on the ERA," in case anyone missed the anti-equality memo from God the first time around. Church leaders at the highest levels officially opposed the amendment.

IF GOOD, INTELLIGENT WOMEN LIKE MY MOM AND GRANDMA HAD BEEN SO PASSIONATELY AGAINST THE ERA, WHY HAD SONIA BEEN FOR IT?

THEY CONDEMNED HER TO... SPIRITUAL DEATH

FOR ADVOCATING FOR GENDER EQUALITY.

Sonia Johnson

Kate Kelly

In the late seventies, it was a race against the clock to get the final three states to ra[...] and Mormons and other conservative religious groups were fighting hard to kill it. T[...] prophet and his two counselors wrote an official statement against the ERA in 1976 [...] it in 1978 in "Reaffirmation of the First Presidency's Position on the ERA," in case a[...] the anti-equality memo from God the first time around. Church leaders at the hi[...] officially opposed the amendment.

Sonia Johnson was a devout Mormon and lived in Virginia when the reaffirmation letter was circulated to local church members. She obediently sat down to read the amendment, expecting to be convinced of its evils and toe the party line just as she had her whole life. But when she read the ERA, she unexpectedly disagreed with the church saying, "I loved it. I just loved it." That was the start of her nationwide quest to get the amendment ratified.

Sonia started the group Mormons for ERA with some of her Mormon ladyfriends in 1978. The group made Sonia the president and spokeswoman, and she was asked to testify at a Senate hearing in favor of the amendment in order to irk its main opponent in the Senate—Orrin Hatch of Utah. During the hearing, Senator Hatch became so visibly upset while questioning Sonia that his rage attracted media attention. Despite his obvious loathing, Sonia continued unruffled and eloquently voiced the sentiments of thousands of Mormon women who, like my mom and grandma, didn't dare speak in favor of the ERA because they had been pressured and intimidated by the church.

Kicking off with a showdown against a powerful senator was the start of many bold actions for Mormons for ERA. They marched down Pennsylvania Avenue with thousands of others in support of ratification. They chained themselves to Mormon temple gates to protest Mormon leadership's political involvement in opposing the ERA. In July 1979, they flew a private airplane towing a huge banner that read RAISE THE FLAG FOR ERA in the sky over the Mormon Temple in Washington, DC, because they knew the wildly conservative Mormon prophet was going to be there for a flag ceremony. These church ladies were *not* messing around. They were radicalized and ready to rock 'n' roll for equality.

These church ladies were not messing around. They were radicalized and ready to rock 'n' roll for equality.

It turns out Sonia Johnson had not disappeared after her excommunication. The (literal) patriarchy had tried their best to dampen Sonia's resolve, but they only solidified it. A year after her excommunication she led a thirty-seven-day fast in Illinois to attempt to convince the legislature to ratify the ERA. With seven other female fasters, she dressed in white and donned a purple sash reminiscent of the suffragists who had fasted in prison. Sonia and her group sat in the Illinois capitol's gallery under the banner WOMEN HUNGER FOR JUSTICE, and fasted for weeks. She was hospitalized three times and became so weak she had to use a wheelchair, but she did not relent. Despite their courageous efforts, Illinois still refused to ratify and her brave crew ended their fast by toasting with grape juice. Sonia declared: "Perhaps we have lost a battle, but we know we are going to win the war." Sonia was catapulted into fame and national feminist leadership. She even ran for president of the United States in 1984. She had a purely feminist platform and a male VP. She came in fifth nationwide and is still one of the only independent candidates to ever qualify for federal matching funds. A pretty far cry from disappearing!

As a result of her activism, Sonia was hauled into a church disciplinary court. Thousands rallied to support her, including secular groups like the National Women's Political Caucus and the National Organization for Women. She had five witnesses testify in her defense at her "trial" and hundreds sent in letters of support. But, in the end, the Mormon men sitting in judgment over Sonia were unpersuadable, and she was convicted of "apostasy," or defying church leadership, and cast out of her community—in their minds, for all eternity. They condemned her to their version of spiritual death for advocating for gender equality.

IN MY CHILDHOOD, THAT'S where the story ended—when Sonia was excommunicated. That was it. Her life, as far as I knew it, was over. When I was young, I prayed to never become so rebellious that I would distance myself from God like she had. Instead, I did everything I was supposed to: I attended Brigham Young University (what Mormons call "the Lord's University"), I was a Mormon missionary in Spain for two years, and I married a man in the Mormon temple in Salt Lake City. Then I went to law school. I crossed my fingers that my piety in other areas would make up for choosing higher education in lieu of motherhood. I took a class in law school on constitutional history and realized for the first time that women really weren't included. In fact, we were actively left out of our own Constitution from the very beginning. I paid rapt attention to the sections of constitutional law about gender discrimination, and I didn't like what I heard. It *still* seemed too easy to pass and keep sex-based discriminatory laws on the books. I questioned why my mom and grandma had spent so much of their time and energy keeping us *out*.

At about the same time I figured out that women weren't in the Constitution, I also came to grips with the fact that women weren't equal in my religion. I learned about why the legal doctrine of "separate but equal" had miserably failed in the United States and why it didn't fly at church, either. So I founded a group called Ordain Women to advocate for gender justice inside the Mormon Church. As a result, I found myself standing in front of the exact same tribunal— ironically called a "Court of Love"—that Sonia Johnson had stood in front of thirty years prior.

Because I lived in the DC area, I was tried in the same building in Vienna, Virginia, that Sonia Johnson had been decades before. Since women aren't permitted to read the rule book by which the proceedings are governed (#patriarchy), my female lawyer had to get a bootlegged copy from WikiLeaks. There was a vigil outside the building while three patriarchs decided my fate.

"I BELIEVE IN WOMEN."

Sonia Johnson

Despite all the community support I got and all that praying I'd done as a kid, I, too, was convicted of apostasy and excommunicated from the church I was trying desperately to make better from the inside. And suddenly, I found myself in the same position as the woman I had thought about with fear and disdain years before. Now that I was an outcast just like Sonia, I set out to meet her and learn more about her side of the story.

When I finally met Sonia in person, I found her living in Arizona with her wife, Jade. I asked about the status of her faith. She said, "I believe in women." That's it. That was my feeling, too. Looking at photos or stages filled with all-male leaders just never felt right. It was like looking at a family portrait where all the wives, mothers, daughters had been erased. We all knew they must have existed, but someone had photoshopped them out. It was a bizarro, womanless version of the universe that we were just supposed to accept. But I never could.

SONIA AND I BOTH fought to make the contributions and the existence of women visible. Like her, once I got a taste of demanding equality, I couldn't stop. I went to my first ERA rally at the US Capitol in 2012, right as I was graduating law school, and I became ERA-obsessed. I wanted to find women like me, throughout history, who felt the same way. Women who believed passionately that equality had to be cemented into our most foundational legal document and wanted to make our country better—from the inside.

I grew up listening to and reading stories about men. The protagonist of every story I heard was a man. In college, I even took a religion course called Teachings of the Living Prophets (who were, of course, all men—hence the need to ordain women). We were required to memorize all the minute details of their lives, including their childhood pastimes, their relationship histories, where and what they studied, their favorite foods— everything. We even had prophet-factoid pop quizzes in class. Over time, and with plenty of indoctrination, I became an expert at seeing things from a man's perspective but not from my own.

Historian Gerda Lerner wrote that there are three stages of writing about women in our histories: First, the compensatory phase, where women existing is acknowledged; second, the contributions phase, where specific ways in which women made contributions are added to male-dominated narratives; and third, when histories center on the women themselves rather than casting them as supporting characters in the histories of men.

I hope *Ordinary Equality* is able to contribute to this third stage, where women are not seen on the periphery of constitution-making, but as Framers themselves. We often say that America was founded on July 4, 1776—but, really, 1776 was just the year a bunch of rich white guys wrote a breakup letter to King George, saying his American colonies were tired of being England's side hustle (the Declaration of Independence). You

There are thousands of women and queer people who contributed to the founding of our country.

know that classic painting of the signing of the Declaration of Independence that's in the US Capitol Rotunda and on the back of the two-dollar bill? It's a room chock-full of men, and they all look like clones. A room full of forty-seven little copies of the same white-wigged avatar. When women insist on the right of our stories being told, we are accused of rewriting history. But that's not true—history has written over us.

I am not a historian; I'm a storyteller. And the story of this amendment is best told through the lives of those who helped shape it and continue to do so. I started the podcast *Ordinary Equality* to help tell their stories. I want these women to be as important to us as prophets. So important that we care about their experiences as young girls, who they rebelled against and what they studied. I want us to memorize the details of the fascinating, adventurous lives they lived. I want you to come to know Molly, Abigail, Phillis, Matilda, Crystal, Alice, Mary, Pauli, Martha, Patsy, Barbara, and Pat and to help carry out *their* prophetic vision for equality.

There are thousands of women and queer people who contributed to the founding of our country and the shaping of our Constitution over time. The visionaries of *Ordinary Equality* are certainly not an exclusive list. But over the last century, there have been many like Helene de Boissiere-Swanson, trekking across America in relentless pursuit of equality. Their stories should be celebrated, not erased.

Mormons have a concept of bearing testimony. It's largely an exercise of listing the things you know to be true in front of the congregation. In this book I hope to list the true stories of my historical heroes and share their living, breathing testimonies of helping to shape our Constitution and the world we now inhabit.

The US Constitution is an imperfect document that even the men who first wrote it admitted would need to change as time went on, and that process is ongoing. One of those still-needed changes is the Equal Rights Amendment. As Helene de Boissiere-Swanson taught me in a rather dramatic manner—women in this country still have many miles to go.

Women and Queer

We the People of the Unite

Article II

HOW TO AMEND THE U.S. CONSTITUTION

ARTICLE V

WE'VE HAD 27 AMENDMENTS &
THEY'VE ALL COME THIS ROUTE

CONGRESS

Pass by 2/3 of the House & Senate

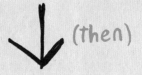 (then)

STATE LEGISLATURES

3/4 (38) state legislatures ratify

THAT'S ALL THE CONSTITUTION REQUIRES!

Then, the National Archivist logs
the state ratifications & publishes
the amendment!

THE ERA IS STUCK AT THIS PART...

MOLLY
BRANT

Koñwatsi-Tsiaiéñni, or Dagonwadonti

1736-1796

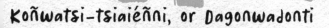

"Where are your WOMEN?"

—Attakullakulla, Cherokee leader

had actually w____ ___ create a truly democratic society where ___, the men wh____ ___ our Constitution had a living, breathi___ ___ave reference ___ front of them. Women had been a___

CHAPTER 1
A BETTER BLUEPRINT

FROM MAY 25 TO SEPTEMBER 17, 1787, fifty-five men met at the Pennsylvania State House in Philadelphia. Their goal: to create a guiding document for the newly minted United States. The final outcome was the US Constitution. The document started with three famous words: "We the People." But, in truth, they intentionally excluded the majority of the people around them. The inalienable rights they laid out in the Constitution covered only white land-owning men like themselves—just 5 percent of the population at the time. That meant that the vast majority of people on this land—women, the poor, enslaved people, and Indigenous Peoples—didn't make the cut. (For obvious reasons.) Each of these groups would have to mount centuries-long social movements to be counted as members of "the People," with constitutional protections, and much of that work remains undone.

The Framers were a select group of some of the wealthiest in the world at the time and their intention was to protect the coinage they had amassed. In other words, the American Revolution was led mostly by the Jeff Bezoses and Bill Gateses of their day. And their wealth was not neutral. (Not even a little bit.) It was amassed primarily by seizing land from Indigenous Peoples and

THEY INTENTIONALLY EXCLUDED THE MAJORITY OF PEOPLE AROUND THEM.

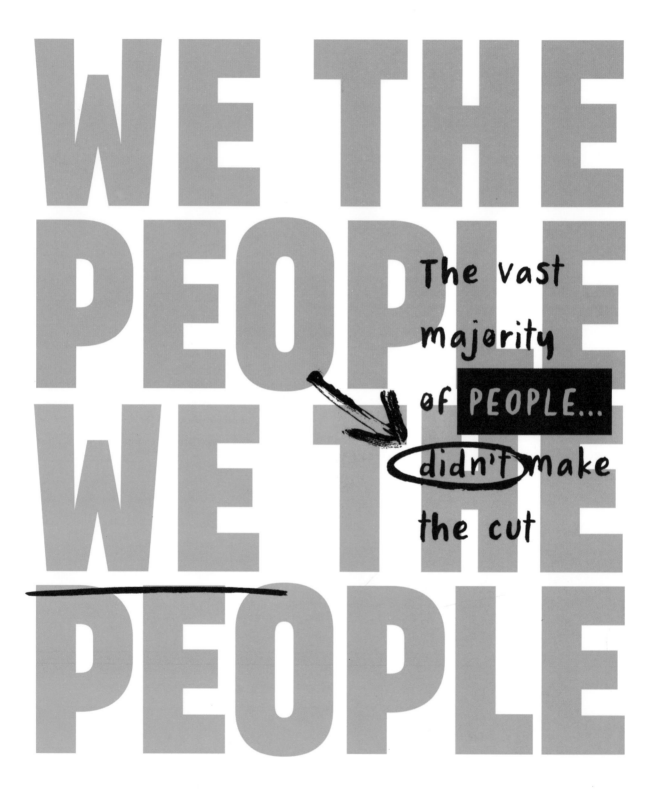

income reaped from the transatlantic slave trade. Many of the Founders were themselves slave owners who literally bought and sold women as property and bred people for profit. So it's not that difficult to figure out why gender equality was never part of their vision for this new country.

If they had actually wanted to create a truly democratic society where women had full equality, the men who drafted our Constitution had a living, breathing example they could have referenced—right in front of them. Women had been a vital part of governance for thousands of years in the neighboring Iroquois Confederacy. But instead, they adopted only the ideas from native governance that consolidated or distracted people from their power grab. (Cultural appropriation on steroids!)

We the (marginalized) people have been dealing with that intentional omission ever since. The reason we need the Equal Rights Amendment is to cash in on that original promise of an inclusive document. This time, we want it to cover all of us. Iroquois leader Molly Brant, or Dagonwadonti, is one example of many strong women who the Founders could have emulated if they had wanted to create a truly equal society.

Women had been a vital part of governance for thousands of years in the neighboring Iroquois Confederacy.

IN UPSTATE NEW YORK, just under three hundred miles from where the Founders wrote the Constitution, the Haudenosaunee were modeling a flourishing democracy with women in high leadership positions. "Iroquois" was the French name given to the Haudenosaunee. They called themselves "People of the Longhouse" because of their traditional lengthy bark-covered longhouses that sheltered many families. They envisioned their government—the Iroquois Confederacy—

The Haudenosaunee's Great Law of Peace or "Kaianerekowa," was the first federal constitution on the American continent and joined the five autonomous tribes together, all the way back in the 1100s. The Great Law introduced a new way of organizing, one of balance. Under this system, the leaders of each clan were not warriors, but rather peace chiefs (or sachem). For every peace chief, there was a female counterpart—a clan mother, or matron.

like a longhouse. It had six different doors, one for each tribe, but once individuals entered, they became one family inside, united. Communal governance modeled after communal living.

The chiefs and clan mothers were very important figures in the community, and were in charge of distribution of resources and stewardship over the land. Approximately one-fourth of the Great Law's clauses recognize the power and influence of Iroquois women.

The US Constitution was heavily influenced by the organizational systems of Native Americans. Benjamin Franklin was particularly well acquainted with Iroquois structures since his publishing house put out translated versions of their treaties and statements about the Great Law of Peace. The Founders of the United States of America used the Iroquois Confederacy as a model for their version of federalism. John Rutledge, a member of the constitutional convention and chair of the drafting committee, used the structure of the Iroquois Confederacy as support for the proposition that political power comes from "We the People."

The Founding Fathers' proximity to native cultures and their direct involvement with native representatives meant that they would have known and seen firsthand the role that women played in native society. Molly Brant is a powerful example of a strong woman who yielded great political power and authority at the time. She was a wolf clan matron. Molly's story illustrates the possibilities our Founders squandered when it came to women's equality and rights.

MOLLY BRANT WAS BORN around 1736 in the Ohio territory. Her parents named her Koñwatsi-tsiaiéñni, which means "Someone lends her a flower." As an adult, following Mohawk custom, she was given the name Dagonwadonti, meaning "She against whom rival forces contend"—truly just an unequivocally badass name.

Molly lived with fellow Mohawks in upstate New York during the Revolutionary War period, which meant she was intimately familiar with a government that practiced radical gender equality. While the Founders were busy investing in patriarchal systems that excluded women from power, the Iroquois were practicing a matrilineal kinship system, where inheritance and social status passed through the maternal line. Clan mothers were essential to their confederation.

Women like Molly had equal representation at tribal councils, where they were able to make consensus decisions with the group. Though the clan mother is the highest official in the Iroquois polity, she's not necessarily the oldest woman in the clan. A

The Cherokee or Aniyunwiya also elevated women to positions of leadership and power. Like women in the Iroquois Confederacy, Cherokee women often controlled the land and negotiated directly with colonial leaders. Women held such powerful and complementary roles in Cherokee society that they could not comprehend a nation that did not honor and enfranchise its women. "Where are your women?" Cherokee leader Attakullakulla asked, baffled when their delegation of Cherokee men and women arrived at a negotiation with English colonists in 1759 and the settlers had zero female representatives.

clan mother is chosen based on her skills in leadership and diplomacy. If a chief were to make decisions the clan mothers did not approve of, they could collectively decide to take his chieftainship away. To fire him, they removed the crown of antlers the chief wore—to literally "dehorn" him. That's some major matriarchal mojo!

The political power of native women was wholly unfamiliar to white women at the time. Many native people saw the newly minted United States as a grossly unequal and dangerous society. Anthropologist Alice Cunningham Fletcher, who studied and documented American Indian culture at the turn of the century, quoted one native woman who said, "As an Indian woman I was free. I owned my home, my person, the work of my own hands, and my children should never forget me. I was better as an Indian woman than under white law." Fletcher even voiced concern about what would happen to native women if they became US citizens—worried that they would be downgraded to the same status as white women (which meant *losing* their rights and being treated with the same legal disrespect—a major demotion). Patriarchy was a foreign concept and an import from Europe that served as a major disservice to native women.

MOLLY BRANT WAS FLUENT in both Mohawk and English and navigated both cultures fluidly. She accompanied her stepfather and a delegation of Mohawk elders to Philadelphia in 1754, the same year the French and Indian War began for control of North America. Because Iroquois women controlled the land, she went to discuss a fraudulent land sale with colonial leaders. Though she was a young woman, her presence in such an important delegation indicated her significant role as a wolf clan matron, a powerful position the colonialists would have taken note of. She must have really challenged those settler stereotypes and was seen as intelligent, proud, and persuasive in an argument—a strong leader with remarkable stamina.

Molly was considered to be quite the catch in her community, but she chose to marry Sir William Johnson, British superintendent of Indian Affairs for the northern colonies and one of the most influential men in North America during the eighteenth century. The marriage was a strategic alliance on both parts due to the importance the Iroquois gave to clan matrons. Despite her European husband,

The societal structure of the Iroquois Confederation so favored women that it even altered the reality of violent crime so common in other societies. Scholars who study the Iroquois have argued that rape was practically nonexistent among the Haudenosaunee prior to white contact. Even their military enemies admitted with surprising candor, "Bad as these savages are, they never violate the chastity of any woman, their prisoner." Of course, this didn't mean violent things never happened in these societies or native men were inherently more benevolent—it meant that the societal structure and incentives favored women, who had power and balance in the community. In many native societies women were too politically powerful to be as vulnerable to sexual assault as white women who had no political power, rights, or even legal identity. There were immediate and severe consequences for disrupting the balance of society in native nations, and this kept the frequency of sexual assault crimes very low.

Sir William Johnson

"MISS MOLLY BRANT'S INFLUENCE OVER [HER PEOPLE] IS FAR SUPERIOR TO THAT OF ALL THEIR CHIEFS PUT TOGETHER."

she continued to wear the clothing of her native tradition and taught her children how to speak both languages and how to traverse both cultures.

The home of Molly and Sir William was the seat of a dozen or more councils with native people between 1759 when they married and 1774 when William died. These councils were attended by hundreds of native leaders and government officials. Since she was both an influential Mohawk wolf clan mother and the wife of Sir William, Molly was in the perfect position to act as mediator between the parties at the meetings. All sides saw her as an important leader and skilled diplomat. Daniel Claus was a British Indian agent and Sir William Johnson's longtime aide and secretary. He was also an avid diarist (what a dream job), and said of Molly, she was "in every respect considered and esteemed by [the Iroquois] . . . and one word from her is more taken notice of by the Five Nations than a thousand from any white man, without exception."

Molly attended an Iroquois Central Council Fire meeting in 1777, just a year after the Declaration of Independence was issued. A Seneca chief, Sayengaraghta, urged all the tribes to take a neutral position and not to side with the British or the Americans in their spat. Molly rose to her feet and boldly denounced the chief. She was completely committed to the British and to what eventually became Canada (a name adapted from the Haudenosaunee word "kanata" which means "village"). Molly asked what the Americans had ever done for the natives, except steal their land. She spoke with such powers of persuasion that she convinced five of the six nations (all except the Oneida) to stick with a previous agreement they had made with the British. One disgruntled American colonel later commented, "Miss Molly Brant's influence over [her people] is far superior to that of all their Chiefs put together."

Had they...
learned from
the existing
societies...
where women
were...an
integral part
of governance...
we wouldn't
even need an
ERA today.

Ten years later in 1787, George Washington presided over the Constitutional Convention. Many of the men at the convention personally knew powerful native leaders like Molly Brant since they had dealt with native women face-to-face in land negotiations. Our Founding Fathers had encountered female leaders in their dealings with native peoples but, during those sweltering days in Philadelphia spent hammering out a document to help found a new nation, they did not even consider a gender-inclusive government. Had they taken the lead from powerful native women like Molly and learned from the existing societies around them where women were valued, safe, and an integral part of governance, perhaps we wouldn't even need an ERA today. Women wouldn't have to be an afterthought now if we had been integrated and included from the get-go, like the Haudenosaunee had in their Great Law of Peace.

NANCY WARD

"Beloved Woman"

The Cherokee or Aniyunwiya also elevated women to positions of leadership and power. Like women in the tribes of the Iroquois Confederacy, Cherokee women often controlled the land and negotiated directly with colonial leaders. Nancy Ward, or Nanye'hi, which means "One who is with the spirit people," was the niece of Attakullakulla and a powerful Cherokee leader who held the office of Ghigau ("beloved woman") in her society.

In 1755, when Nancy was just eighteen years old, the Cherokee had an intertribal conflict with the Muscogee Creeks. During the battle, Nancy was assisting her first husband, Kingfisher. When he was mortally wounded, Nancy reportedly took up his rifle and joined the fight. She went on to lead her people to victory. Due to her bravery and leadership, the Cherokee gave her the title of "beloved woman." The title made Nancy a member of the tribal council of chiefs, and she served as an adept peace negotiator and ambassador for the Cherokee people.

In 1781, Nancy was tasked with speaking before a crowd of male US treaty officials to defend her people and their land. She was so commanding that she let this group of powerful men—who did not believe that women should have any political leadership roles—know that she regarded them as children who were below her in authority, saying, "We are your Mothers; you are our sons. Our cry [is] all for Peace; let it continue because we are Your Mothers. This Peace must last forever. Let your Women's sons be Ours, and let our sons be yours. Let your Women hear our Words." Nancy admonished them to see women as their equals.

ABIGAIL ADAMS

"I desire you would **Remember the Ladies,** and be more generous and favourable to them than your ancestors. Do not put such unlimited power into the hands of the Husbands. Remember all Men would be tyrants if they could."

1744–1818

As an adult, Abigail didn't slow down in the slightest. She advocated for girls, arguing that they should be allowed to attend public schools along their ma... peers, saying "I regret the trifling narrow contracted Education of the... les of my...

bigail was such a close advisor to her husba...
ounder" of the United States, even thoug...
ly participate in any of the proceeding... n Adams was
hiladelphia as a delegate to the Continental Congress, he wrote
to his wife back home in Massachusetts telling her, "I
without you!" "You must come! You must come!" and

CHAPTER 2
MRS. PRESIDENT

DESPITE COMING FROM a prominent family, Abigail Adams never received any formal education, a fact she lamented throughout her life. "I never was sent to any school . . . Female education in the best of families went no further than writing and arithmetic." Rather, she learned to read and write from her mother and grandmother and took to writing letters at an early age. When her brother went to Harvard, she borrowed his books to study things girls were not permitted to and taught herself French by reading plays. She was like a sponge and soaked up any lessons she could through her informal studies. Her quick wit and aptitude for correspondence later came in handy when she wrote hundreds of letters filled with counsel to her husband, the president.

As an adult, Abigail didn't slow down in the slightest. She advocated for better education for girls, arguing that they should be allowed to attend public schools alongside their male peers, saying, "I regret the trifling narrow contracted Education of the Females of my own country." She made sure to educate her own children, including her daughter Nabby, even when their formal schooling was interrupted by the tumultuous times they lived in. Abigail became a cheerleader for the kind of education she was so upset to have missed out on.

"I REGRET THE TRIFLING NARROW CONTRACTED EDUCATION OF THE FEMALES OF MY OWN COUNTRY."

FOR MANY OF THE Founding Fathers, there was a fight for equality happening not on any battlefront, but very close to home. Their own wives were pressing them to make women equal citizens with equal rights. One of those women was Abigail Adams, wife of John Adams, the prominent Founder and later president. Born Abigail Smith, she was part of a well-established, wealthy family in Massachusetts. Later, she passed on her mother's maiden name, Quincy (not her own surname Smith), to her firstborn son and future president—in order to keep her family's matrilineal line alive. Ahead of her time in many ways, she was always thinking of tactics for women to circumvent the rules and customs that served to further their oppression.

Abigail and John were apart for much of their married life due to the travel his political activities and diplomatic mission to France required. (International travel in those days could be a months- or even years-long undertaking.) The couple kept up a robust correspondence, writing over eleven hundred letters over the years. They often teased each other and had serious conversations couched in jokes. Both were great at the colonial version of throwing shade, and often called each other "saucy," meaning cheeky or full of sass. And Abigail Adams was, indeed, very lively. She was not afraid to speak her mind in her letters or to advocate for herself or her sex. One time early in their marriage, she wrote John, asking, "Don't you think me a Courageous Being? Courage is a laudable, a Glorious Virtue in your Sex—why not in mine?" It seemed foolish to her to assign gender even to virtues.

Abigail was such a close advisor to her husband that some consider her a "Founder" of the United States, even though she was not permitted to formally participate in any of the

As a leader of the Revolution, John Adams was in a key position to help determine who got rights in the newly formed United States of America—and who did not. On March 31, 1776, just months before the Declaration was finalized and published, Abigail wrote to John in Philadelphia where the Congress was meeting:

In the new Code of Laws which I suppose it will be necessary for you to make I desire you would Remember the Ladies, and be more generous and favourable to them than your ancestors . . . Remember all Men would be tyrants if they could. If particular care and attention is not paid to the Ladies we are determined to foment a Rebellion and will not hold ourselves bound by any Laws in which we have no voice, or Representation.

[And then Abigail Adams laid the ultimate smackdown.]

That your Sex are Naturally Tyrannical is a Truth so thoroughly established as to admit of no dispute, but . . . Men of Sense in all Ages abhor those customs which treat us only as the vassals of your Sex.

proceedings. When John Adams was away in Philadelphia as a delegate to the Continental Congress, he wrote daily letters to his wife back home in Massachusetts telling her, "I cannot do this without you!"; "You must come! You must come!"; and "Come, I can't do this!" To say he relied heavily on her advice is an understatement. Lucky for him, she had plenty of wise counsel to give.

As was customary at the time, due to limited paper and letter-writing supplies, Abigail would often write a few words, then strike through them to delete and start again on the very next line of the same page. In much of her writing that survives, it seems she was thinking through her arguments as she wrote them (stream-of-consciousness style). But in her "Remember the Ladies" letter, now one of her most famous pieces of writing, Abigail never second-guessed. She's so steadfast on the page it's likely she and John and others—perhaps her sisters, Mary and Elizabeth, or the many luminaries she kept as pen pals—had had this conversation before.

Even though John Adams loved and respected his wife, he scoffed at her appeals for equality. His smart-aleck response was:

REMEMBER ALL MEN WOULD BE TYRANTS IF THEY COULD.
—Abigail Adams

Abigail Adams

John Adams

The petticoats were indeed ready to revolt!

As to your extraordinary code of laws, I cannot but laugh . . . Your letter was the first intimation that another tribe more numerous and powerful than all the rest were grown discontented. This is rather too coarse a compliment, but you are so saucy, I won't blot it out . . . [We] know better than to repeal our masculine systems . . . We have only the name of masters, and rather than give up this, which would completely subject us to the despotism of the petticoat, I hope General Washington, and all our brave heroes would fight.

As you might expect, Abigail Adams was *not amused* by John's joke about the "despotism of the petticoat" in the slightest. She immediately rage-texted her BFF Mercy Otis Warren (via letter) to vent her frustration, writing, "He is very saucy to me in return for a List of Female Grievances which I transmitted to him." Abigail later added, "I think I will get you to join me in a petition to Congress." The petticoats were indeed ready to revolt!

Sadly, we don't know what, if anything, became of that scheme to conspire together for women's rights. But Abigail was so aware of her influence on the Continental Congress as they set about drafting the Constitution that she gave herself the title "Mrs. Delegate." In one letter to John, she wondered what he would think of her claiming such a title but then mused, "Why should we not assume your titles when we give you up our names[?]" (Touché, Abigail!)

––––––––––

ABIGAIL ADAMS WAS NOT only concerned about the condition of women, but also about inequality in all its colonial manifestations. She was particularly outspoken against slavery. Abigail had grown up in a household with four enslaved people since her father was a slave owner, but, unlike the majority of the other Founders, she and John never owned any people. While they employed servants, the Adamses paid them a fair wage and championed education for all their staff. In fact, slavery was legally abolished by the Massachusetts Constitution in the 1780s, which was largely drafted by John himself. "I wish most sincerely there was not a Slave in the province," Abigail wrote in 1774. (It is important to note, though, that later the Adamses did live in the White House, which was being constructed using slave labor while they occupied it, and they benefitted indirectly from slavery in other ways.)

In Boston on July 18, 1776, Abigail joined a crowd to hear the Declaration of Independence read publicly for the first time (the eighteenth-century version of being the first person to see a breaking-news tweet). She was irate that not only were women excluded, but also that the final publication of the Declaration was missing the denunciation of slavery she knew the drafting committee had originally included. These men, many of whom she knew personally and cared for, had profoundly disappointed her. Once they had cemented their own power, the writers of the Constitution put women in a position

In the great democratic experiment that was the United States there were pockets of progress on the gender front. From 1776 to 1807, women in New Jersey had equal voting rights, demonstrating Abigail Adams and her contemporary crusaders were right: women were capable of participating as equals in governance.

The Founders adopted the legal concept "feme covert" or coverture, imported from the common law of England, which literally means "covered woman." Under coverture, a married woman didn't have a separate existence from her husband and could not own any property, make contracts, or sign legal documents. She could not make a contract with her husband, because that would be like a husband making a contract with himself. The first law that gave married women property rights didn't pass until 1839 in Mississippi—an ordinance that was modeled after the tribal customs of the Chickasaw Indians. Yet again, native women paved the way for equality.

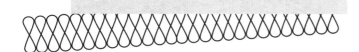

of political subordination even more severe than they had been in the colonial period before it.

FOR HER ENTIRE ADULT life, Abigail Adams would continue to challenge the world around her, especially the traditional ideas about women. She believed that women should be allowed to vote and to hold public office, and she was always willing to cut her husband down to size. When John became the second president of the United States, people referred to Abigail as "Mrs. President" or the "Presidentress" because of her assertion of her own power and position. In many ways, she was a feminist before the term was even invented!

The Founders selectively borrowed from native governance structures to draft an exclusionary version of a Constitution, but women like Abigail Adams took their own inspiration from native women, like Molly Brant, who had full control of their personal property in their own societies. Abigail even made an unusual move for a woman of her time and wrote her own will. But because of coverture, the will had no real legal force, and Abigail appealed to the good nature of her husband to carry out her wishes. She modeled the change she wanted to see for American women, literally, until her dying day. For Abigail Adams, writing out that four-page handwritten document was a final act of rebellion. And with it, she claimed her own power—even in death.

Of course, Abigail Adams wasn't the only American woman who dramatically influenced the path of the country. Some women participated in the war directly as soldiers, like Deborah Sampson, who became a hero of the American Revolution when she disguised herself as a man in order to join the Patriot forces. Others, like Esther de Berdt Reed, organized women to collect funds in support of the revolution. And while the quieter contributions of many have been lost to history, Abigail wanted these women to be remembered. In her epic "Remember the Ladies" letter, she argued women should take revolutionary action. "Our ambition is kindled by the fame of those heroines of antiquity. . . . If opinion and manners did not forbid us to march to glory by the same paths as Men, we should at least equal, and sometimes surpass them in our love for the public good. I glory in all that which my sex has done great and commendable."

MERCY OTIS WARREN

Revolutionary Playwright

Mercy Otis Warren was a celebrated poet, historian, and political satirist (she loved skewering the British!), and playwright during the American Revolution. Married to James Warren, president of the Massachusetts Provincial Congress, she mingled in impressive circles, and often exchanged letters with both John and Abigail Adams. In fact, she was so prolific in her letter writing that she is known as an acclaimed epistolary author (#goals). Ever the contrarian, she was always willing to speak her mind—which made her the perfect person for Abigail to complain to when John was annoying her—and in those days if you had a good zinger of a letter, it was often published, so many of her letters made it to print.

Mercy had no formal education but was a voracious reader and gifted writer. Her 1788 pamphlet, *Observations on the New Constitution*, authored under a gender-neutral pseudonym, would become a major influence on the Bill of Rights—so, in a very meaningful way, she was a female Framer, too. She published her plays and poems under her own name, but unfortunately because she lived in Puritan Boston (bummer), staging plays was a no-go, and none were ever performed live.

Following the success of her pamphlet, she wrote a full history of the American Revolution, *History of the Rise, Progress, and Termination of the American Revolution*, the only book of its kind by a woman. In it Mercy wrote, "It may be a mistake, that man, in a state of nature, is more disposed to cruelty than courtesy." Fluke of nature or not, Mercy had no patience for cruel or lackluster men, and she encouraged all to join the revolution.

In order to be taken seriously, women often had to write under male pen names—just like women today who are forced to use male avatars or handles online to avoid harassment and gender bias. For example, the Brontë sisters published their novels *Jane Eyre*, *Wuthering Heights*, and *The Tenant of Wildfell Hall* under the pseudonyms Currer (Charlotte), Ellis (Emily), and Acton (Anne) Bell.

Mercy Otis Warren

WHEATLEY

PHILLIS

"In every human breast, God has implanted a Principle, which we call Love of Freedom; it is impatient of Oppression, and pants for Deliverance."

In 1773, Phillis Wheatley, the first African American and enslaved person to publish a book of poetry with the support of the family who owned her, the Wheatleys, and they took her to England to show off an extraordinary journey for an extraordinary woman. Though she was enslaved, Phillis made an impressive book of poetry with the

CHAPTER 3

GENIUS IN BONDAGE

IN 1773, PHILLIS WHEATLEY took her first trip abroad, an extraordinary journey for an extraordinary woman. Though she was enslaved, Phillis had written an impressive book of poetry with the support of the family who owned her, the Wheatleys, and they took her to England to show off her talents and find a patron and publisher for her book.

In London, she met many influential people, including Benjamin Franklin and the Lord Mayor of London, who gifted her a copy of John Milton's *Paradise Lost*. She also found a patron in Selina Hastings, Countess of Huntingdon, who was known as "Lady Bountiful" because of all the cash she shelled out for religious and philanthropic causes. The countess helped Phillis get her book published.

Poems on Various Subjects, Religious and Moral was the first book of poetry ever published by an African American woman— a remarkable feat. And thanks to an English court case (*Somerset v. Stewart*) the previous year that ruled slavery was against British law and interpreted to mean no enslaved person brought to England from the colonies could be compelled to return as one, Phillis was able to secure her own official emancipation during her British tour.

THE FIRST BOOK OF POETRY EVER PUBLISHED BY AN AFRICAN AMERICAN WOMAN

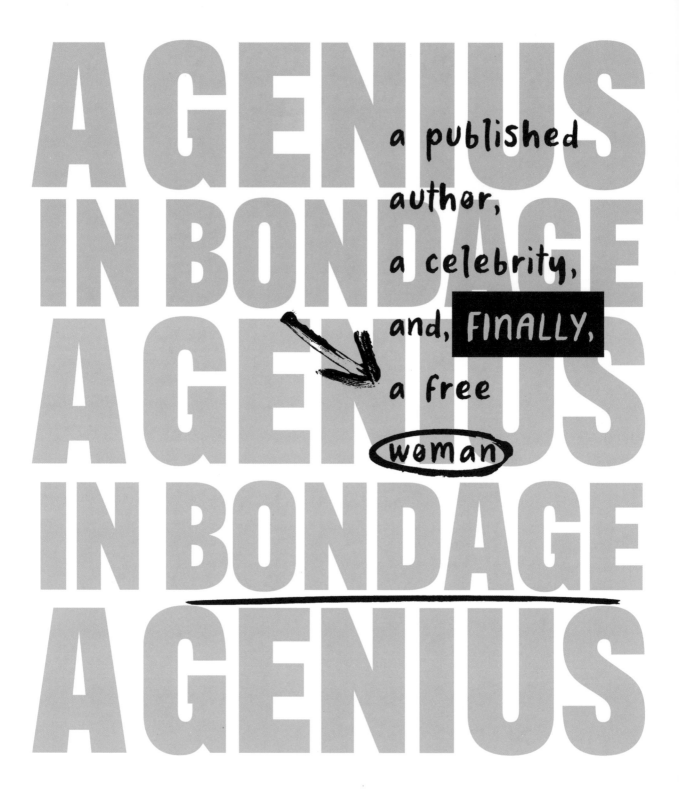

A GENIUS
IN BONDAGE
A GENIUS
IN BONDAGE
A GENIUS

a published
author,
a celebrity,
and, **FINALLY**,
a free
woman

At the age of nineteen, Phillis Wheatley was a published author, a celebrity, and, finally, a free woman.

DURING THE AMERICAN REVOLUTIONARY period, one-fifth of all people in the United States were enslaved. There would have been no vast property acquisition and no amassing of colossal fortunes in the newly forming United States without the kidnapping, exploitation, and enslavement of Africans and their descendants. The fortunes of many of the Framers of the Constitution were tied up in the enslaved people they owned. Four of the first five US presidents amassed their wealth from the slave-breeding industry, not cash crops from large plantations. The prosperity of many in the North, even if they didn't own slaves outright, was facilitated by the commerce of the Northern ports, like those in New York or Baltimore, which were kept busy by the transatlantic slave trade. If you were rich anywhere in colonial America, you were almost invariably implicated in the slave trade.

As historian and author Dr. Rebecca Hall puts it, the Constitution was "an affirmative action document for slaveholders and slave breeders." The document crafted at the Constitutional Convention in 1787 set up an elaborate system to exclude enslaved people from full personhood. At the same time, the Framers conceived of a way to count enslaved people to boost their population and to give Southern slave owners more power so that they would agree to the Constitution. These

Instead of electing the president by popular vote, the Electoral College let each Southern state count its slaves, albeit with a two-fifths decrease, in computing its share of voting power. This allowed slave states to maintain disproportional influence over the presidential election but still not let any enslaved people actually vote.

The Constitutional mandate, known as the Fugitive Slave Clause, is the first and only time the Founders used the pronoun "she" in the Constitution (whereas "he" is used throughout). "If any person bound to service or labor in any of the U—States shall escape into another state, he or she shall not be discharged from such service or labor . . . but shall be delivered up to the person justly claiming their service or labor."

dastardly concessions were accomplished through the so-called Three-Fifths Compromise and the creation of the Electoral College. The Constitution also, for the *first time*, issued a mandate that free states return "fugitive" (runaway) slaves back into slavery and paved a more profitable path for slave-breeding states.

The exclusion of women and their pronouns from the Constitution was no accident. The Founders knew women existed, but as many historical women knew all too well, the men just didn't want to acknowledge women as anything but property—and enslaved women like Phillis Wheatley were using every opportunity they had to fight the system of chattel slavery that the US Constitution helped solidify and facilitate.

PHILLIS WHEATLEY ARRIVED IN

Boston on July 11, 1761. Born in Western Africa, likely Senegal or Gambia, she was kidnapped when she was around six or seven years old and brought to the American colonies on a slave ship called the *Phillis*, which is how she inherited her first name—a lifelong reminder of that harrowing journey. Susanna Wheatley, the wife of prominent Boston tailor John Wheatley, purchased Phillis "for a trifle" because she was so weak the captain of the ship thought she was terminally ill, and he wanted to profit off her before she died.

As a very devout Congregationalist, Susanna felt it was the Wheatley's duty to teach Phillis to read the Bible. As Phillis progressed and showed great aptitude, she was also tutored in English literature, geography, astronomy, mythology, and Latin. Since most enslaved people were forbidden to learn how to read and write—and very few women of any race were that well educated—Phillis's life was an anomaly. She rose in the dark every morning so that she could write her poetry before starting her domestic chores, and it soon became apparent she had a natural talent for writing. Her first published work, in a Rhode Island newspaper at age twelve,

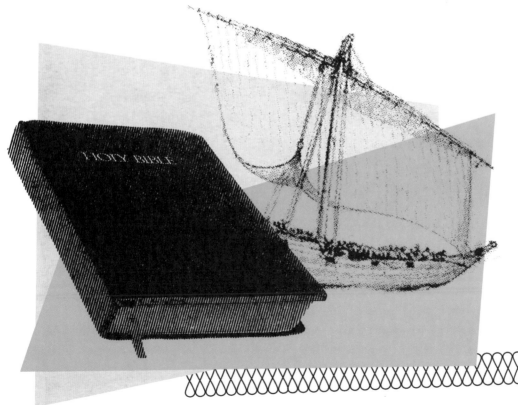

Her book *Poems on Various Subjects* became a bestseller of the day and reached the upper echelons of colonial society thanks in large part to its preface that featured seventeen prominent Bostonian men—including John Hancock and the governor of Massachusetts—asserting that they believed Phillis was indeed the author. As an enslaved woman, she had to have men vouch for her to have any credibility.

quickly earned her renown in Boston for her education, writing ability, and skill. Phillis was a prodigy. Yet, she remained the property of the Wheatley family despite their unusual support for her writing career. The Black British writer Ignatius Sancho admired her writing and was outraged Phillis was still enslaved. He called her a "Genius in bondage" when her book of poems was published.

LIKELY DUE TO THE biblical education Phillis received from the Wheatleys, religion was a key influence and a prominent thread throughout her work. She was also a strong supporter of the American Revolution and penned several poems in honor of the Continental Army's commander, George Washington. (Yep, *that* George Washington.) After Washington, who himself became a slave owner at age eleven when his dad died, received one poem Phillis sent to him, he invited her to visit him at the army's headquarters in nearby Cambridge, Massachusetts. She accepted his invitation and had a private audience with General Washington in March 1776, just four months before the Declaration of Independence was issued.

Other fans of Phillis among the day's elite were the philosopher Thomas Paine, who published one of Phillis's poems in the *Pennsylvania Gazette*, and Dr. Benjamin Rush, one of the signers of the Declaration of Independence. While Phillis was committed to the revolutionary cause, she was not down to actively participate in her own oppression. She believed that independence from the British was a righteous cause, but that the pernicious evil of slavery prevented the colonists from achieving true heroism. As a victim of slavery herself, it wasn't something she was willing to overlook.

After she secured her own manumission, because she had been enslaved herself and was then a newly freed Black woman in a very precarious situation, Phillis wasn't at liberty to directly speak against slavery. In her writing, she often used cleverly applied biblical symbolism to comment on the slave trade. In her best-known poem, "On Being Brought from Africa to America," Phillis reminds readers that Black people were going to be their eternal equals in heaven: "Remember, Christians, Negroes, Black as Cain, / May refin'd and join th' angelic train."

In a letter to her friend Reverend Samson Occum, a native Mohegan author and

In the country's early years, Christian groups played a large role in the governance of each of the British colonies, and both enslavers and abolitionists alike approached Phillis's religious work with very different aims. (Black women's work being co-opted is nothing new.) The former used it to try to convince the enslaved population to convert to Christianity and accept their subjugation as God's will, whereas the latter saw it as proof of the intellectual abilities of people of African descent adding to the reasons they should be freed.

FINALLY, A FREE WOMAN.

John Peters

Phillis Wheatley

"THE EXERCISE OF OPPRESSIVE POWER OVER OTHERS AGREE I HUMBLY THINK IT DOES NOT REQUIRE THE PENETRATION OF A PHILOSOPHER TO DETERMINE."

ordained Presbyterian minister, Phillis condemned the hypocrisy of the slave owners (or "modern Egyptians," as she called them) and their "love of Freedom." She called out the "strange Absurdity of their Conduct whose Words and Actions are so diametrically opposite," and speculated that "the Cry for Liberty, and the reverse Disposition for the exercise of oppressive power over others agree I humbly think it does not require the penetration of a Philosopher to determine." In other words—you're a bunch of hypocrites, and you don't have to be all that smart to see it.

After her initial success, Phillis continued to write, but her condemnation of the slave trade, the growing tensions with the British, and the onset of the Revolutionary War weakened public enthusiasm for her poems. She was never able to publish a second book. During her years of writing, she received emotional support and advice from her friend Obour Tanner, an enslaved woman in Rhode Island with whom Phillis maintained correspondence throughout her adult life. They could uniquely support and understand each other. Their continued survival and resistance, despite an elaborate system designed to extract everything from them, was a testament to their strength.

In her piece addressed "To the Right and Honourable William, Earl of Dartmouth," Phillis declares a love of freedom rooted in her own experience as a slave:

No more, America, in mournful strain /
Of wrongs, and grievance
unredress'd complain, /
No longer shalt thou dread
the iron chain, /
Which wanton Tyranny with
lawless hand /
Had made, and with it meant t'
enslave the land. /
Should you, my Lord, while you
peruse my song, /
Wonder from whence my love of
Freedom sprung, /
Whence flow these wishes
for the common good, /
By feeling hearts along
best understood, /
I, young in life, by seeming cruel fate /
Was snatch'd from Afric's
fancy'd happy seat . . .

Throughout the colonies, slave masters constantly feared their slaves would revolt, and with good reason. In 1775, the royal governor of Virginia issued a proclamation offering freedom to all enslaved people if they fought on the British side in the Revolutionary War. Thousands of enslaved women made good on the British decree to grant freedom to any who defected to the Loyalist cause, and records show that single mothers with as many as four or five young children fled their masters to join the British. In all, tens of thousands of enslaved people escaped, including an estimated twenty-five thousand in South Carolina, thirty thousand in Virginia, and almost one-quarter of the enslaved population in Georgia.

ON APRIL 1, 1778, despite the skepticism and disapproval of some of her closest friends, Phillis Wheatley married a fellow free African American from Boston, John Peters. Peters was considered very elegant and dashing, but did not have luck in business. Like many recently freed from enslavement, Phillis and John found themselves constantly battling poverty, and she had to work as a maid in a Boston boardinghouse to support them. Their marriage was a struggle, and although she bore three children, all died in infancy.

Eventually Phillis was even forced to sell her treasured volume of *Paradise Lost* that she had received all those years before in order to help her husband pay his debts. Margaretta Matilda Odell, a relative of Susanna Wheatley's, recalled, "[Phillis] was reduced to a condition too loathsome to describe. . . . In a filthy apartment, in an obscure part of the metropolis. . . . The woman who had stood honored and respected in the presence of the wise and good . . . was numbering the last hours of life in a state of the most abject misery, surrounded by all the emblems of a squalid poverty!" Without having ever been able to realize her dream of earning

a living as an author, Phillis Wheatley was in her early thirties when she died on December 5, 1784, due to complications from childbirth.

Despite its lamentable end, Phillis's life was a testament to the genius and capabilities of women, specifically Black women. She overcame seemingly insurmountable setbacks, rising above to directly influence the thinking of so many of the men who wrote our Constitution. As a survivor of the transatlantic slave trade, she spoke out eloquently against it. These words she used to describe a friend of her original patron Countess of Huntingdon in a poem were certainly true of her, too: "Thou didst, in strains of eloquence refin'd, Inflame the soul, and captivate the mind."

...Petition... Belinda Sutton of Boston...
...humbly sheweth, that your petitioner...
...duction of... service for a long... years...
...the hon.ble Isaac Royall...
...Resolve of the honourable General...
...of fifty two dollars per Annum...
...begs leave further to represent to...
...honours that three years of the...
...now due to her therefore she begs that...
...Money would be pleased to Issue a Warra...
...to the Treasurer of this Commonwealth in...
...the sum of One hundred & fifty six Dollars...
...account as aforesaid and as in...
bound Your Petitioner will Ever pray____

Boston March 13th 1788

Belinda X Sutton
her mark

BELINDA SUTTON
The First Call for Reparations

In the 1780s, an enslaved woman named Belinda Sutton (Royall) was left by her British master when he fled to England after the British were defeated in the Revolutionary War. The newly victorious Americans seized his property and freed all his slaves but left them to fend for themselves. Belinda successfully petitioned the Massachusetts state legislature for back wages as reparations from her former master's estate.

Her petition contains one of the first known accounts of the Middle Passage from Africa to America as told by an enslaved woman. Published in a Philadelphia magazine in 1787, the petition recounts that the Africans aboard her ship were "suffering the most excruciating torment; and some of them rejoicing that the pangs of death came like a balm to their wounds." She signed the petition with an X, indicating that she was probably unable to read or write.

Shockingly, even though the deck was stacked completely against her, Belinda won her case. She was awarded an annual income of fifteen pounds and twelve shillings from her former master's estate. Unfortunately, she had a helluva time collecting on the judgment. Belinda's petition for a pension is seen as the first call for reparations for slavery in the United States.

MATILDA
JOSLYN
GAGE

1826-1898

"A REBEL! How glorious the name sounds when applied to woman. Oh, rebellious woman, to you the world looks in hope. Upon you has fallen the glorious task of bringing liberty to the earth and all the inhabitants thereof."

As a young girl, Matilda Joslyn Gage would ... friends, neighbors, and even strangers to make antislavery petitions around ... freedom for a ... they thought that opinions should be formed on the basis of logic ... or religion. ... da credited her training in the abolition movement to her organ ... advocacy skills. "I have frequently been asked what first turned my thoughts tow ...

... Joslyn Gage would ... ... nds, neighbors ... ... lieved in ... ... asi ... ... n th ... ... requ ... ... hts

CHAPTER 4
THAT WORD IS LIBERTY

AS A YOUNG GIRL, Matilda Joslyn Gage would take antislavery petitions around her town, asking friends, neighbors, and even strangers to sign them. Both of Matilda's parents believed in freedom for all. They thought that opinions should be formed on the basis of logic, not tradition or religion. Matilda credited her training in the abolition movement to her organizing and advocacy skills: "I have frequently been asked what first turned my thoughts toward woman's rights. I think I was born with a hatred of oppression, and, too, in my father's house, I was trained in the anti-slavery ranks."

She used the skills she learned in the abolition movement in her fight for women's rights. When she was just fifteen years old, Matilda publicly questioned the all-male leadership of a local church. Her dad, who was away for medical training, sent a supportive letter to her mother. He always stood by his daughter and defended her right to speak up. Matilda later said, "If there has been one education of more value to me than all others, it was the training I received from my father to think for myself."

"I THINK I WAS BORN WITH A HATRED OF OPPRESSION."

THAT WORD
IS LIBERTY

THAT WORD
IS LIBERTY

THAT WORD
IS LIBERTY

"I was _trained_ in the **ANTI-**slavery ranks."

BORN MATILDA ELECTA JOSLYN in upstate New York in 1826, she was raised in an abolitionist home that was an active station on the Underground Railroad. Her father, Hezekiah, let her participate in all the meetings held at their house, which was very unusual for a child at the time. The neighbors were appalled by her confidence and insistence that she be heard publicly. (Not to mention her door-knocking for causes—an outright scandal for a girl in those days.)

Matilda's father raised her in other unconventional ways, too. Being the area's only medical doctor, he taught her many subjects forbidden to women, including physiology and anatomy. As his only child, Hezekiah's dream was for Matilda to also become a physician, and he even took her on his medical rounds to neighboring communities. Women were not allowed to go to medical school at the time, but they hoped the rules would change by the time Matilda was old enough.

She had worked for years to prepare to become a doctor, and her father wrote letter after letter trying to get her admitted to any medical school he could, hoping that his recommendations could get

Her middle name was prescient and also somewhat ironic for what would become her life's work—helping women to participate in elections. "Electa" means "chosen one" in Greek, and the second epistle of John in the New Testament mentions a woman named Electa and commends her and her family "for their steadfastness in the true faith and exhorts them to persevere." The biblical reference made the name popular in early America—but Matilda would eventually turn against Christianity and organized religion quite spectacularly.

The Seneca Falls Convention was really a regional event, which was held there because it's where activist Elizabeth Cady Stanton lived at the time, and she and Lucretia Mott had been the organizers of the gathering. The convention emerged as nationally important only after the fact, because it was there they adopted the Declaration of Sentiments—their bold woman-ifesto that outlined their priorities and demands and put the idea of women's suffrage out there in print for the first time, a wildly radical position in 1848.

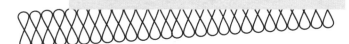

her accepted, despite the fact women were still banned from studying medicine. He solicited help from anyone he could think of, including his alma mater, but the answers always came back a firm no. Matilda was devastated. Barred from medical school and practice, she opted instead to become a teacher. At the age of eighteen, she met a supportive and reform-minded young store owner named Henry Gage and the two were married.

In 1848, having just given birth to her first child, Helen Leslie, Matilda was unable to attend the first-ever American women's rights convention held in mid-July of that year in nearby Seneca Falls, New York, but she paid rapt attention to it. From that moment, Matilda was "united in it heart and soul" with the other women and followed news of the fledgling movement as it grew. When the third national women's rights convention was held in 1852, this time even closer to her in Syracuse, New York, she went with her toddler in tow. At just twenty-six years old, Matilda was the youngest person to address the convention.

Although she was no stranger to public speaking, Matilda was soft-spoken and had never addressed a group anywhere near as large, but she always rose to challenges. Ready to up the ante on the appreciation of women, her speech gave a shocking retelling of history outlining women's contributions throughout the ages. She felt strongly that women needed knowledge of their past, not only of their oppression, but the achievements and victories, too. She was "trembling in every limb" as she spoke, but Matilda's speech ended with a rousing call: "Fear not any attempt to front down the revolution . . . nothing is a more fertile aid of reform, than an attempt to check it; work on!" To her absolute delight, suffrage star Lucretia Mott so loved what she'd said that she decided to publish the speech, and from that moment on Matilda hitched her star to the women's rights movement.

In 1870, she published the pamphlet "Woman as Inventor" in order to bring to light the achievements of women that had been lost to history, explaining how their contributions had been erased most frequently by being misattributed to men. While others liked to highlight what women could do, Matilda consistently pointed out what women had *already* done, and she's considered to be the first bona fide women's historian.

Men taking credit for women's work was a constant outrage for Matilda Joslyn Gage, and she took every opportunity to call it out. Nearly a century after Matilda's death in 1993, science historian Margaret W. Rossiter coined the term the "Matilda Effect," named after her, to describe men being credited for women's scientific contributions and ideas. For example, Nettie Stevens discovered XY sex chromosomes, but she didn't get credit—solely because she had two Xs. Nettie's male colleague E. B. Wilson is often erroneously cited as the one who discovered sex chromosomes, because . . . well . . . of his sex.

Susan B. Anthony

Matilda Joslyn Gage

Elizabeth Cady Stanton

MATILDA JOSLYN GAGE BECAME

one of the most well-known suffragists of her time. She, Susan B. Anthony, and Elizabeth Cady Stanton were the ultimate suffrage triumvirate. Elizabeth Cady was a theoretician and Susan B. was an activist, but Matilda was both, and she led some of the movement's boldest actions. In Philadelphia, on July 4, 1876—the nation's centennial celebration—Matilda, along with Susan B. and Elizabeth Cady, issued a list of articles of impeachment against the entire US government for denying women equal rights. The suffrage leaders stormed the stage at the celebration, and Susan B. handed their accusations directly to the vice president of the United States in front of the crowd. They stated that the history of our country had been "a series of assumptions and usurpations of power over woman, in direct opposition to the principles of just government," including in part the "natural rights of each individual," the "equality of [those] rights," that "no person can exercise the rights of others without delegated authority," and that "the non-use of rights does not destroy them." (Talk about guts!) They accused the government of violating "these fundamental principles of our government" and called for impeachment.

EVEN THOUGH IT WAS illegal, Matilda attempted to vote in 1871, and as a result of breaking the voting law, she was arrested. She remarked upon her arrest, "All the crimes which I was not guilty of rushed through my mind, but I failed to remember that I was a born criminal—a woman." Susan B. Anthony later managed to successfully vote in 1872 but was also arrested shortly after. Having been through this ordeal already, Matilda went to Rochester to help her prepare for her trial. She wrote Susan B.'s speech "Is It a Crime for a U.S. Citizen to Vote?" and together they went on a speaking tour of the county to get their views out to the public (and to the potential jury pool) before the trial. Even these two powerful organizers were no match for misogyny, and Susan B. was convicted. She refused to ever pay her fine.

By 1880, women who owned property in New York were able to convince the legislature that they should be allowed to vote in the school district elections where they paid taxes. Matilda had been preparing the women in her town for weeks, and when there was an election just three days after the vote was approved, Matilda was the first in the line of all 102 women to—finally—vote legally. Casting her ballot for the first time, the local newspaper described her as the "happiest woman in America."

Although now able to vote in some municipal elections, women still couldn't vote in federal ones, and so they kept making their discontent known. In 1886, a large gift from France to celebrate American independence was scheduled to be unveiled in New York. Matilda was vice president of the New York State Woman Suffrage Association (NYSWSA) at the time, and the group petitioned to speak at the unveiling of the Statue of Liberty. Ironically, President Cleveland, who opposed women's suffrage,

"I WAS A BORN CRIMINAL— A WOMAN."

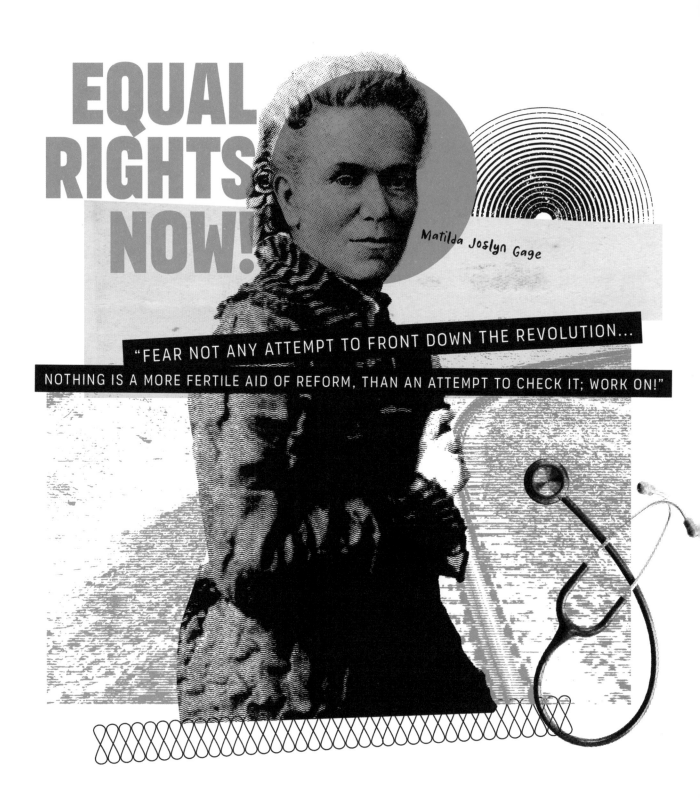

EQUAL RIGHTS NOW!

Matilda Joslyn Gage

"FEAR NOT ANY ATTEMPT TO FRONT DOWN THE REVOLUTION... NOTHING IS A MORE FERTILE AID OF REFORM, THAN AN ATTEMPT TO CHECK IT; WORK ON!"

was scheduled to speak at the dedication event. To keep them quiet, the men in charge not only denied women the opportunity to speak, but they also refused to even let any women on the tiny island where the statue is located. (Talk about getting voted off the island!) Matilda proclaimed it was "the sarcasm of the 19th Century to represent liberty as a woman, while not one single woman throughout the length and breadth of the land is as yet in possession of political liberty!"

Outraged by this blatant injustice, Matilda and NYSWSA President Lillie Devereux Blake decided to protest. Since women were barred from stepping foot on the island, they staged their demonstration on the water. The only boat they could find to rent was a cattle barge, but the captain promised to clean it out before the women got on board. They held rallies and sold tickets in order to pay for the rental. It was a terribly blustery day on October 28, 1886, but the women were determined not to let Lady Liberty go up without publicly pointing out the irony that women couldn't vote in France, where the statue was from, or in the United States. So two hundred women (and twenty-five men) boarded the ship—which the captain had *not* cleaned out—and unfurled their VOTES FOR WOMEN banners. They held their noses and shouted into megaphones, chanting "Equal rights now!" and "Change the Constitution!" As they got closer to the island, their captain steered the barge front and center, stopping directly under the copper statue. All the news coverage of the event included the women and their demands, so it was considered a rousing success—and well worth the stink!

Matilda's daughter Helen Leslie Gage, who was a toddler at the first women's rights convention she'd attended, was thirty-two years old in 1880. When women in New York cast their ballots in their school district elections, Helen was voted onto a local school board as the first-ever female clerk. Not only did Matilda finally get to vote, but she also got to vote for her own daughter!

IN ADDITION TO BECOMING one of its boldest activists, Matilda was a prolific author and intellectual architect of the suffrage movement. She started a newspaper called *The National Citizen and Ballot Box*, and said: "Women of every class, condition, rank and name will find this paper their friend." An original consciousness raiser, she used her words to help wake women up and explained, "As the first process toward becoming well is to know that you are ill, one of the principle aims of the National Citizen is to make those women discontented who are now content," a goal that made many conservatives across the country howl in protest.

The suffrage movement had two nationwide primary associations: the American Woman Suffrage Association (AWSA) based out of Boston and the National Woman Suffrage Association (NWSA) based mainly out of New York, to which Matilda and the rest of the triumvirate belonged. The two groups were so at odds that they would not even mention or acknowledge each other publicly. AWSA was more conservative, its ranks filled with more religious temperance movement ladies who wanted the vote so they could achieve prohibition, enforce prayer in schools, and amend the Constitution to literally recognize Jesus Christ as "the author and head of government," and favored a state-by-state approach to gaining suffrage. NWSA was more radical and openly spoke out against religion as a source of oppression for women and insisted on a national suffrage amendment, refusing to wait for each state to approve.

Despite this conflict of interests, Susan B. Anthony thought it would be a strategic advantage for the two groups to merge to build the ranks of the suffrage movement. In order to shut down opposition, she blocked the main critic of religion, Matilda, from attending the 1889 convention by denying her funds to travel. After most delegates had left, Susan B. held a vote to merge the groups. (Please note the hypocrisy of not letting members of a *suffrage organization* vote!) She then placed people loyal to her in all the offices of the newly combined organization, the National American Woman Suffrage Association (NAWSA), and according to Matilda, "steered [the] organization into an orthodox pit-hole." The NWSA had been an organization of equals, but the merged NAWSA quickly became a hierarchy, with Susan B. Anthony and the younger women who were loyal to her (called her "nieces") as its only leaders. As a result, the national suffrage movement as a whole became more conservative.

In the area around Syracuse, New York, where Matilda grew up, white settlers and native people lived closely and relatively peacefully. Local newspapers reported on events in both communities, and as she aged, her childhood interest in her native neighbors grew. In 1875, she wrote a series of articles about how the Six Nations of the Haudenosaunee (Iroquois) Confederacy shared power equally between men and women for the *New York Evening Post*. In 1893, Matilda was given an honorary adoption into the Mohawk Nation's wolf clan, the same clan as Molly Brant (page 1). Matilda was given the name Karonienhawi, which means "She who holds the sky." She was later admitted into the Haudenosaunee Council of Matrons, which gave her full voting rights—something she did not enjoy in her own nation's government— a stark contrast that was not lost on her.

Matilda was blindsided by the betrayal by her closest friends and fellow suffragists. She wrote, "I never met so much deceit, vilification, animosity and all uncharitableness as I found . . . among my former co-workers." The sting of what Susan B. and Elizabeth Cady had done to her would never dull. Even worse, many historians attribute this move to a decades-long lull in the suffrage movement, referred to as the "doldrums," when the quality of activism went down and forward movement completely stalled.

EVEN THOUGH MUCH OF her energy was spent working for the vote, Matilda never saw suffrage as the end goal. A complete upending of the patriarchy was her ultimate aim. She believed that the subordination of women was not peripheral to Christianity but was its centerpiece—the belief that had gotten her booted from the NWSA—and viewed liberating women from organized religion as a natural next step in her fight. In a speech years earlier at the 1878 Freethinker's Convention in

MATILDA NEVER SAW SUFFRAGE AS THE END GOAL. A COMPLETE UPENDING OF THE PATRIARCHY WAS HER ULTIMATE AIM.

Watkins Glen, New York, Matilda said, "Christianity is a political religion"—an insight that feels relevant to today's fight for equal rights. This idea came to fruition in her 1893 magnum opus, *Woman, Church and State*, a scathing critique of organized religion's part in the oppression of women, in which she set out to disprove the myth that God had designed the subjugation of women in order to inspire women to draw their own conclusions from historical events. Although it was a radical book, it was well received at the time, getting favorable reviews in many papers, including the *New York Times*. Russian author Leo Tolstoy even sent her a letter full of praise, which included this backhanded compliment: "It proved a woman could think logically."

THE ORGANIZED FIGHT FOR a women's suffrage amendment took seventy-two years—from July 19, 1848 to the final ratification of the Nineteenth Amendment on August 16, 1920. Not one of the early pioneers of the movement lived to see its eventual success, but Matilda knew they were "battling for the good of those who shall come after us; they, not ourselves, shall enter into the harvest." She always had an eye on the long arc of women's history.

For many years, Susan B. Anthony, Matilda Joslyn Gage, and Elizabeth Cady Stanton (and then later Ida Husted Harper), had been working on a book called the *History of Woman Suffrage*. These women saw themselves as constitution-makers—even collecting official versions of their signatures for posterity, like the men who had signed the Declaration of Independence—and they wanted to ensure an accurate history of their legacy was

In 1890, after decades of partnership with the NWSA, Matilda left to organize the Woman's National Liberal Union. The new organization had a newspaper called *The Liberal Thinker*. In its only issue she wrote, "This government of the people, by the people, and for the people seems to be very much limited in the interpretation of the word people; the poor, the women, both married and single, the children, the Indians and other unfortunate inhabitants are not people; the phrase should be changed to read, a government of rich men by rich men, for rich men."

recorded. But Susan B., in true Mean Girl fashion, also used *History of Woman Suffrage* to write women she didn't like out of the story of suffrage—including one of its coauthors. Susan B. lived eight years longer than Matilda and spent that time deleting most of the references of her from the book before the final volume was published.

This erasure of historical women—the very thing Matilda had fought so hard throughout her life to correct and prevent—meant that her vital role as one of the most important members of suffrage was lost to time (which might be why we don't have any coins or statues dedicated to Matilda Joslyn Gage today like good ol' Susan B.). But throughout all life's adversity, Matilda never lost her boldness. It seemed that challenges made her even stronger. She was so firm in her beliefs and committed to proclaiming them, that she had the following carved on her tombstone at the Fayetteville Cemetery in New York:

THERE IS A WORD
SWEETER THAN MOTHER, HOME
OR HEAVEN
THAT WORD IS LIBERTY

VOTES FOR WOMEN

Seneca Falls

Morning Post.

MATILDA THE GOOD WITCH

A Feminist Oz

Luckily there were those who remembered Matilda Josyln Gage's greatness, including her family. Her youngest daughter, Maud, following in her mother's romantic footsteps, was married to author L. Frank Baum in a ceremony that was lauded as "one of equality" by a local newspaper, which noted that promises from the bride and the groom were "precisely the same."

Baum was a playwright who told fantastical stories to entertain his kids and the neighborhood children. They were so wonderful that his mother-in-law constantly encouraged him to write them down. Those stories would later become *The Wonderful Wizard of Oz*, and Dorothy, the independent, curious, and confident protagonist, was inspired by Matilda. Baum's biographers also routinely assert that he borrowed the concept of the Good Witch wholesale from Matilda's writings.

Baum went on to write thirteen more Oz books, and Matilda's influence pervades the entire series. She had written in her book *Woman, Church and State* that "ma," the etymological root for the word "mother" is

Aryan for "creator." And this idea surely inspired the second book in the series, which features the issue of women's rights as a central theme. In it, the women of Oz, frustrated with their second–class status, form an army led by a female general and take over the land. Since the male characters—the Wizard and the Scarecrow—had failed to keep the peace, Princess Ozma and Glinda the Good Witch decide to establish what Matilda referred to in her work as a "matriarchate" and rule the kingdom together. For the rest of the series, Oz is a feminist utopia, ruled by women, just as Matilda would have envisioned.

Maud Baum

L. Frank Baum

CRYSTAL

EASTMAN

can begin." Of course, she was right.

right is over! But women, if I know them, are saying, 'Now at last
the fight is over! But women, if I know them, are saying, 'Now at last
vote, she wrote: "Men are saying perhaps 'Thank God, this everlas-
ment was ratified in 1920, after years of personally fighting for the
fight for equal rights for women, and when the Nineteenth Amend-
She knew that gaining suffrage was just the very beginning of the

"Feminists
are not
nuns.
We want
to love
and to be
loved."

1881-1928

throughout her life, her "rad
ventional lifestyle got Eastm
some to call her the "most
America." At one point she
three different governme

CHAPTER 5
THE MOST DANGEROUS WOMAN IN AMERICA

AT NEARLY SIX FEET tall Crystal Eastman was a magnificent presence in any room. Known for her forthright opinions and formidable debate prowess, she was a force of nature in every discussion she was a part of. It was said of her, "when she spoke to people—whether it was to a small committee or a swarming crowd—hearts beat faster and nerves tightened as she talked." You did not want to be on the receiving end of a Crystal Eastman verbal battering, but thankfully she used her oratory skills to unrelentingly fight for equality.

She knew that gaining suffrage was just the very beginning of the fight for equal rights for women, and when the Nineteenth Amendment was ratified in 1920, after years of personally fighting for the vote, she wrote: "Men are saying perhaps 'Thank God, this everlasting fight is over!' But women, if I know them, are saying, 'Now at last we can begin.'" Of course, she was right.

SHE USED HER ORATORY SKILLS TO UNRELENTINGLY FIGHT FOR EQUALITY.

CRYSTAL EASTMAN WAS BORN in Glenora, New York, in 1881. Her parents, Samuel Eastman and Annis Bertha Ford, met at Oberlin College, where her dad was studying to be

a minister and her mom a teacher. Annis followed her calling instead of teaching and in 1890, she became one of the first women ordained as a Congregational minister in New York. She even had her own church. This was practically unheard of for a woman at the time, and no doubt had a lasting effect on Crystal's views of women in positions of power. Crystal said of her, "When my mother preached we hated to miss it. . . . Her voice was music; she spoke simply, without effort, almost without gestures, standing very still. And what she said seemed to come straight from her heart to yours." Annis was a renowned preacher and at one point (as an early adopter of male feminist allyship) Crystal's dad even served as co-pastor to his wife. The pair made a dynamic duo.

Religious life was not very lucrative, and money was always tight while Crystal was growing up. Parishioners and friends provided financial assistance and often lent money to the family. They also hosted boarders in their house, who contributed to the family's well-being. Crystal said, "There were always clever, interesting, amusing women coming in and out of our house." This mix of independent, intelligent visitors helped expose her to unconventional feminist ideas growing up.

Women were seen as equals in her family, and Crystal was allowed and encouraged to speak her mind. When

The family's commitment to gender equality didn't stop at their front door. They spent summers on the shores of Seneca Lake in Upstate New York, and one summer, Crystal prepared a sixteen-point brief in support of the girls removing their stockings while swimming. Her dad was the kind of man "that was a suffragist from the day he first heard of a woman who wanted to vote." He was persuaded by her rationale and defended her from the scorn of neighbors who were outraged to see girls "naked" (up to their knees) swimming—the scandal! Crystal recalled many years later, "I think it shocked him to his dying day. But he himself had been a swimmer; he knew he would not want to swim in a skirt and stockings. Why then should I?" (I think we can safely say Samuel Eastman deserved the 1890s Dad of the Decade award!)

she was young, she complained that as the only girl she should not have to perform just stereotypical "women's work." As a result, her parents distributed tasks on a gender-neutral basis. If she had to make her bed, so did her brothers. If there was dishwashing to be done, the boys had to take their turns, too. Crystal declared that there was "no such thing as boys' work and girls' work" in the family—which she never regretted, even when she had to do her fair share of wood-chopping and outdoor chores. A close friend said of her, "You wouldn't believe her freedom—she was entirely free, open, full of joy in life."

Crystal never rode sidesaddle, as was the custom for women at the time. She careened around her hometown "on a man's saddle in fluttering vast brown bloomers" that shocked everyone. Those who knew her well described her as a passionate woman who never sought male approval. Friends called her a "tigress." Her brother, Max, said from the time she was very young the family referred to Crystal as a "mighty girl."

The Eastmans were always engaged in intellectual conversations and elaborate leisure activities. They often held symposiums on different topics, and at one held during the summer when Crystal

NOW AT LAST WE CAN BEGIN.

Crystal Eastman

"SHE WAS FOR THOUSANDS A SYMBOL OF WHAT THE FREE WOMAN MIGHT BE."

IT'S NEVER TOO EARLY TO BECOME A FULL-FLEDGED FEMINIST.

was fifteen, her mother instructed her to read a paper called "Woman," her first taste of formal feminism. She wrote that women "must have work of their own because the only way to be happy is to have an absorbing interest in life which is not bound up with any particular person"—prescient words for such a young person—and she dedicated the rest of her life to just that. Many years later as an adult, she said she knew basically all she needed to know to be an effective feminist as a young woman: "I read a paper on 'Woman' when I was fifteen, and I believe I was as wise in feminism then as I am now, if a little more solemn." Proving it's never too early to become a full-fledged feminist.

CRYSTAL GRADUATED FROM HIGH school in 1899 and launched into adulthood in a new century. She attended Vassar Female College, where she met one of her best friends and fellow feminist, Lucy Burns (page 76). Crystal excelled in college. Wherever she went, she "was the most intelligent person in the room." After graduating from Vassar in 1903, she went on to receive a master's in sociology from Columbia University.

With her love of debate and fighting injustice, law school seemed like a natural next step, but she was initially apprehensive about pursuing a law degree. To get a taste of the real thing, Crystal visited court twice and upon seeing practicing lawyers in action, she decided, "There is nothing to be afraid of, and . . . I can be as good at it as the next man." She entered New York University law school in 1906. She found law frustrating at times, and after taking her final exams wrote to her mother, "I hope I passed but I'm not a bit sure. I forgot many of the maddening little reasonless rules." But, she persevered.

Crystal was one of 16 women in a class of 156 and many of her male classmates didn't think she deserved to be there. But like a 1900s Elle Woods, she showed them, and in 1907—after completing her degree in a single year—she graduated from law school second in her class. (What, like it's hard?)

Even as a top graduate with proven potential, and one of only three women to be admitted to the New York Bar, Crystal was unable to find a job as a lawyer because she was a woman. This was a crisis for her for many reasons, but most of all because she found practicing law incredibly fulfilling and threw herself completely into every cause. A true workaholic, she hated rest and inactivity. Despite health issues due to a childhood bout with scarlet fever, her work energized her and she never slowed down.

Her love of work also translated to love of the working class. Since she couldn't find a job as a lawyer in New York, she took one in Pittsburgh doing the first comprehensive study of the causes of workplace accidents and their consequences. In 1910, her work led her to publish an article and then a book called *Work Accidents and the Law*, which argued that the deck was stacked against workers who had been injured on the job. Unfairly kept from practicing law in the traditional sense, Crystal found a way to revolutionize the law in the area of workers' compensation within only a few years. And never one to think small or set her sights low, Crystal then decided to use her legal training not to advocate for individual clients in a courtroom, but to change the US Constitution.

Suffragists were battling for equality state by state, but between 1896 and 1910, none had caved and extended them the vote. These years came to be known among suffragists as "the doldrums." The movement had stalled, and nothing was . . . moving. This was due, in part, to Susan B. Anthony's conservative coup of NWSA, the largest suffrage organization (page 48).

EVEN BEFORE SHE KNEW the term, Crystal Eastman was a feminist, but the next chapter of her life drew her directly into the national spotlight on the struggle for women's equality. Perhaps ironically, it was a man who led her to shift her focus from workplace safety to women's suffrage. In 1910, she fell in love with an incredibly handsome insurance salesman from Milwaukee named Wallace "Bennie" Benedict. Her brother, Max, said of Bennie, "He was one of those rare males . . . who like to have the woman they love amount to something." (May none of us ever settle for less!) They married at New York City Hall and soon moved to Wisconsin. Incredibly close with her family, particularly Max, Crystal was not eager to leave New York, but she followed her heart—and career opportunities.

The following year was a critical moment in the long struggle for women's suffrage. In 1907, while Crystal was a law student, she and her friends had started to shake up the languishing feminist movement by using more radical, confrontational tactics.

In 1911, California suffragists broke the losing streak and won suffrage in that state! Buoyed by the California victory, in 1912, referendum campaigns for women's suffrage were launched in six states, including Wisconsin. Having recently moved there, Crystal was recruited as the campaign manager of the Wisconsin Political Equality League and dove head-first into leading the state's campaign for suffrage.

Anna Howard Shaw, the president of National American Woman Suffrage Association (NAWSA), the combined organization that Susan B. Anthony had maneuvered into being, said of Crystal, "She is a live, splendid little woman who will touch some live wires and set things going." And she did. While the national suffrage groups were being accused of racism, an early intersectional feminist, Crystal made a herculean effort to organize and unite different suffrage groups of all races in Wisconsin. She was very intentional about reaching out to Black women and corresponding with Mary White Ovington, the principal cofounder of the National Association for the Advancement of Colored People (NAACP) about racial outreach efforts. Sadly, powerful beer brewers in the area had conducted a well-organized and well-financed campaign against suffrage, and the Wisconsin bid for suffrage was unsuccessful. Unfortunately, Crystal's

"SHE IS A LIVE, SPLENDID LITTLE WOMAN WHO WILL TOUCH SOME LIVE WIRES AND SET THINGS GOING."

marriage was also unsuccessful, so—now hooked on women's rights—she went back to New York, single again.

––––––––––

AFTER HER STINGING DEFEAT in Wisconsin, Crystal Eastman wanted to try a totally new and less frustrating approach to suffrage than the laborious state-by-state campaign she'd been helping wage. She was ready to shake things up, which naturally led her to reconnect with her old partner in crime, Lucy Burns, and new friend Alice Paul. The youngsters were impatient for "rights we should have won [already] in the nineteenth century" and the group was able to persuade the NAWSA to promote a federal constitutional amendment. They dubbed it the "Susan B. Anthony Amendment" to help gain approval. The older, more demure leaders of the NAWSA weren't really paying attention to the federal strategy at that point, so they let the new Crystal-Alice-Lucy triumvirate start the radical Congressional Union for Woman Suffrage. They didn't think the strategy would amount to much, but never underestimate radical young women with a score to settle!

In 1913, Crystal threw herself into the work of their newly created Congressional Union, giving hundreds of speeches for suffrage, organizing fundraising events, lobbying members of Congress, and doing a tour of demonstrations and speeches in Pennsylvania, Ohio, Indiana, Wisconsin, Minnesota, North Dakota, Montana, and Wyoming. She said, "Indifference is harder to fight than hostility," and she was anything but indifferent—she was on fire. Because of increasing pushback from the old guard as their work started getting attention, they eventually split off from the suffrage fuddy-duddies and formed the National Woman's Party (NWP)—the first women's political party in the world—and

Crystal served on the executive committee. The party completely revitalized the struggle for women's equality. Crystal wrote, "The American woman suffrage movement was born again. Suffrage was no longer a dull and rather obvious reform which our mothers and grandmothers had worked for. It had been dramatized for us. It was a glorious fight worth of our best mettle." (Spoiler alert: The NWP is the group that actually pushed suffrage over the finish line, and then became the main group that would fight for the ERA for the next fifty years.)

When all was said and done and the Nineteenth Amendment was ratified in 1920, the same people who had been scandalized by Crystal Eastman and her friends' militant suffrage tactics claimed the victory as their own. (Stay tuned: We'll hear more about the wild things they did in the chapter about Crystal's coconspirator, Alice Paul on page 97!) Crystal clapped back at "those who had scorned and condemned when the pickets stood for months at the White House gates, when they insisted on going to jail and starved themselves when they got there—all these came now with their wreaths and their flowers and their banners to celebrate the victory." She was really *not* having it with the hypocrites who had fought them every step of the way, and then wanted to claim their sacrifices in victory. Nice try, haters.

"Suffrage was no longer a dull and rather obvious reform. . . . It was a glorious fight worth of our best mettle."

AFTER THE RATIFICATION OF the Nineteenth Amendment, women everywhere were in the streets celebrating the momentous victory. But never one to rest on her laurels, Crystal rocked up to the stage with a speech titled "Now We Can Begin." In it she said that no matter how hard they had all worked, suffrage was the first step, not the last. "In fighting for the right to vote most women have tried to be either non-committal or

"FREEDOM IS A LARGE WORD."

thoroughly respectable on every other subject. Now they can say what they are really after—in common with all the rest of the struggling world—is freedom. Freedom is a large word."

She also spoke out against the disenfranchisement of Black women and the race discrimination that would continue even after the Nineteenth Amendment was ratified. Her post-suffrage-amendment feminist agenda was extensive, race-conscious, and international in focus. It's wild to think that the one-hundred-year-old feminist agenda is so woefully similar to what we're still fighting for today.

In order to accomplish her first objective, "equality under the law," Crystal went back to her law school roots. In 1921, she, along with other seasoned suffragists, began consulting with the NWP and Alice Paul to draft the original Equal Rights Amendment. Crystal acknowledged it would be an uphill climb, though in retrospect, perhaps underestimated the amount of opposition.

In 1924, the year after the ERA was introduced, she said, "The principle of the Equal Rights Amendment is supremely important. The very passion with which it is opposed suggests that it is vital. To blot out of every law book in the land, to sweep out of every dusty court-room, to erase from every judge's mind that centuries-old precedent as to woman's inferiority and dependence and need for protection, to substitute for it at one blow the simple new precedent of equality, that is a fight worth making even if it takes ten years." She understood its vital importance but—whew!—what she thought would take a decade still isn't done a century later.

THE NEWLY PRINTED ERA was unveiled in Seneca Falls, New York, in 1923 at the 75th anniversary celebration of the first women's rights convention (the one Matilda Joslyn Gage had heard about but missed due to childbirth). Almost immediately, the "equalitarian feminists" and women's labor reformers became staunchly divided. Eastman had been on the side of laborers since early in her career, but ultimately she was a radical feminist who believed—above all—in equality. Famous social reformers like Jane Addams and Florence Kelley wanted to keep labor laws they had fought for that protected female workers, but Crystal saw such laws as cruelly discriminatory because they regulated working conditions for women only. She said, "To this sort of interference with her working life the modern woman can have but one attitude: I am not a child. I will have none of your protection." If something protected women *only*, it put them on a pedestal, which Crystal knew even then served only to limit their options—under the guise of support.

She recoiled at the court cases that upheld these women-only laws because they relied on

In 1920, after winning the battle for the Nineteenth Amendment, Crystal Eastman outlined the new feminist agenda:

1. Equality under the law
2. Breaking down barriers to entry of professions to women including equal pay
3. Equal housework for men and women
4. Control of reproductive capacity ("voluntary motherhood")
5. Economic independence and security
6. Compensation for unpaid labor

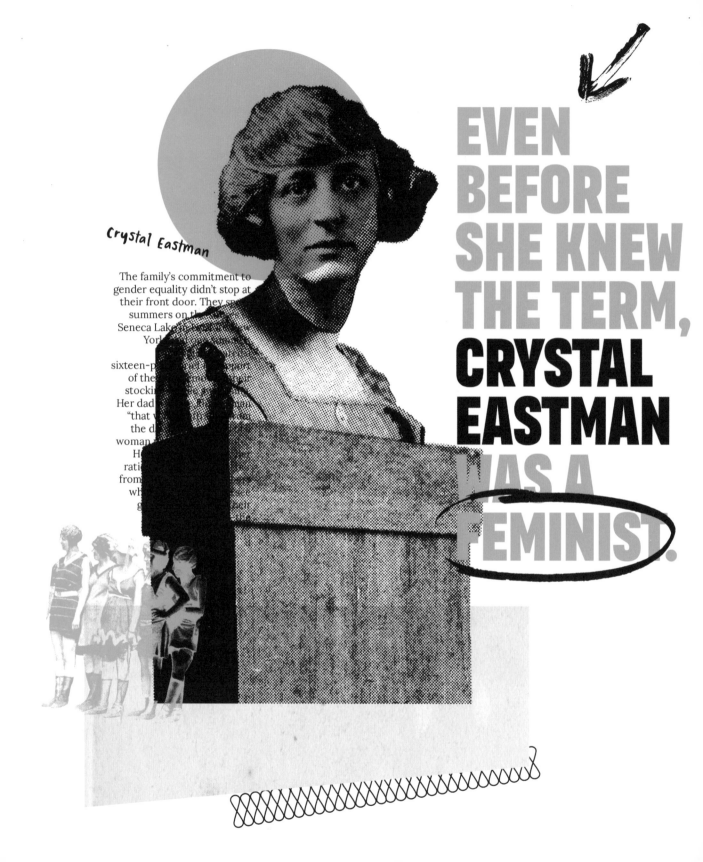

Crystal Eastman

The family's commitment to
gender equality didn't stop at
their front door. They s...
summers on t...
Seneca Lake...
Yor...

sixteen-p...
of the...
stocki...
Her dad...
"that v...
the d...
woman...
H...
rati...
from...
wh...
g...

EVEN BEFORE SHE KNEW THE TERM, CRYSTAL EASTMAN WAS A FEMINIST.

demonstrating that women were physically inferior and needed protection—something Crystal was never willing to concede and vehemently opposed enshrining in case law. For her, protecting workers was a humanitarian cause and had nothing to do with the specific needs, rights, or aspirations of women. In fact, she knew that often claims of protection are used to dress up attempts to set women back. She maintained that these "protective" labor laws that focused solely on women actually kept women out of lucrative trades and positions. Crystal knew these were pink-washed arguments that, at the end of the day, only served to keep women out of the Constitution, and she was not having it. She continued to passionately push for the ERA.

ONE MIGHT THINK THAT serving as a leader of one movement is enough, but not Crystal Eastman. As an ardent pacifist, she strongly opposed the First World War, and in 1915 she cofounded, along with her frenemy, Jane Addams, and other prominent reformers, the American Union Against Militarism (AUAM) and served as its first director. In 1916, Crystal's efforts to start a massive publicity campaign helped avert a war with Mexico. Afterward she said, "We must make it known to everybody that people acting directly—not through their governments or diplomats or armies—stopped that war, and can stop all wars if enough of them will act together and act quickly." She took the words "government by the people" very literally.

Crystal consistently spoke out against the horrors of violence at home and abroad. She wrote for a publication called *Four Lights* and in 1917 spoke out against the race riots in East Saint Louis, saying, "American Negroes have died under more horrible conditions than any noncombatants who were sunk by German

Crystal Eastman invited Claude McKay, one of the leading poets of the Harlem Renaissance, to write for the publication *The Liberator*. When they met, he said, "The moment I saw her and heard her voice I liked Crystal Eastman. I think she was the most beautiful white woman I ever knew . . . her beauty was not so much of her features . . . but in her magnificent presence." They became lifelong friends, and he carried a note from her with him as inspiration and a memento for many years, later weeping as he read it for the last time when he learned she had passed away.

submarines." She saw people of color as her equals, and decried the racism of some of her feminist colleagues.

That same year, 1917, Crystal, Roger Nash Baldwin, and Norman Thomas created a new AUAM project—the National Civil Liberties Bureau (NCLB) to fight government suppression of dissenters' rights during World War I and represent those arrested under the new Espionage Act. Her brother, Max, who was then the editor of a radical socialist newspaper called *The Masses*, was one of the people being prosecuted under the new law that the group sought to protect. Her fellow suffragists were also being arrested, beaten, and imprisoned for exercising their free speech rights in order to get the vote, so she had many personal reasons to want to protect dissent.

In 1920, Crystal had two big wins: the suffrage movement triumphed, and the NCLB was reconstituted as a new organization—the American Civil Liberties Union. The ACLU was largely her brainchild, but was then usurped by Roger Nash Baldwin (who she had initially brought into the project) when she was bedridden on maternity leave in a hospital in New Jersey after a difficult pregnancy.

Though Crystal had been its architect, specifically of the test-case approach that became the signature strategy of the ACLU, Baldwin inserted himself as the leader of the organization against her will, right when Crystal was most vulnerable. By the time she got out of the hospital months later, his name was already on the organization's letterhead, and it was too late for her to reassert control. (Booo hisss, Roger!)

THROUGHOUT HER LIFE, her "radical" views and unconventional lifestyle got Crystal Eastman in trouble, leading some to call her the "most dangerous woman in America." At one point, she was under surveillance of three different government agencies: the Secret Service, military intelligence, and the emerging FBI. She was also placed on a Daughters of the American Revolution watch list of "doubtful speakers." She spoke frequently and publicly about access to birth control. She saw absolute bodily autonomy as the beginning, not the end, of women's rights. "Feminists are not nuns. We want to love and to be loved . . . But we want our love to be joyous and free—not clouded with ignorance and fear. And we

Under Baldwin's leadership, the ACLU—the organization Crystal had conceptualized and founded—did not even support her Equal Rights Amendment. It didn't change its position until 1970, when board member Dorothy Kenyon changed her mind and worked with Pauli Murray (page 119) to advocate for support of the amendment. Had Crystal been in charge, they would not have missed out on those many decades of ACLU backing the amendment.

Crystal Eastman was also a vocal proponent of "free love," a movement at the time that taught sexual matters were the concern of the people involved and not the state. Though she was married twice to men, she lived a radical lifestyle and wrote about it. One of her most famous pieces, 1923's "Marriage Under Two Roofs," caused quite a stir. In it, she admitted she and her husband did not live together, and argued that having "two roofs" offered greater autonomy for women, which created stronger, happier families and love lives. "Ahead of her time" doesn't even cut it—a radical opinion, even by today's standards—she's still ahead of our time.

want our children to be deliberately, eagerly called into being, when we are at our best, not crowded upon us in times of poverty and weakness. We want this precious sex knowledge not just for ourselves, the conscious feminists; we want it for all the millions of unconscious feminists that swarm the earth—we want it for all women." Crystal encouraged women to live as they wanted to, unbound by social expectations, and force the culture to catch up with them.

CRYSTAL CONTINUED TO BE one of the most ardent supporters of the Equal Rights Amendment and served as a bridge between different groups that supported the ERA until her early death in 1928 at the age of forty-six. She pushed for revolution to the end saying, "All we ask is that humanity should find ways and means for the permanent realization of sex-equality." Her last thoughts were of her children and also—showing the true dedication to her vocation—all the work she still had left to do. A friend wrote at the time, "She was for thousands a symbol of what the free woman might be." In her obituary, Freda Kirchwey wrote, "Crystal Eastman . . . carried with her the breath of courage and contagious belief in the coming triumph of freedom and decent human relations. These were her religion . . . She believed in absolute equality . . . She saw in the light of her faith a world in which men and women worked and played and loved as equals; nothing less than this would satisfy her."

"FEMINISTS ARE NOT NUNS."

LUCY BURNS
Spitfire Suffragist

Lucy Burns was a fierce Catholic suffragist from Brooklyn with bright red hair that matched her fiery personality. She was so feisty that she was once described as "worth her weight in wild cats." Crystal Eastman was a year behind Lucy in college, and she was immediately drawn to the older girl. After meeting her, she excitedly told her brother, "Oh my! I like that girl."

The two became more like siblings than friends and got into all kinds of trouble at Vassar, which was a very liberal campus in every respect—except when it came to suffrage. When the male college president forbade any discussion of votes for women on campus,

Lucy and Crystal were undeterred and organized suffrage meetings just beyond the campus grounds in a cemetery.

A brilliant student, Lucy went to study at Oxford College in England. It was there she learned to match her brash personality with bold, militant action. In England, Lucy was arrested repeatedly for suffrage demonstrations and protesting, and she went to prison four different times.

While in jail in London, Lucy met Alice Paul for the first time. Alice approached Lucy because in a sea of British inmates, she was wearing an American flag pin. They helped each other survive prison, and together brought their militant suffrage tactics back home to the United States. It was Lucy who introduced Alice Paul to Crystal Eastman, and the history-making militant-suffragist alliance between them flourished.

Lucy Burns

MARY CHURCH

TERRELL

1863-1954

"A white WOMAN has only one handicap to overcome—that of sex. I have two—both sex and race. I belong to the only group in the country which has two such huge obstacles to surmount."

Like her parents, Mary believed in quality education for Black children. In 1887, after receiving her bachelors and masters degree before the age of twenty-five, Mary moved to

CHAPTER 6
LIFTING AS WE CLIMB

MARY CHURCH TERRELL WAS an excellent student who spoke five different languages—English, French, German, Latin, and Greek—and was a voracious reader. But her academic pursuits were accented by her sheer love of dance. Her passion for movement was inextinguishable, even though it was seen as unladylike by her college, no matter how many languages you could speak.

Mary recounted, "It was against the rules for girls to dance at any of the college functions, and decidedly against the rules for young men and women to dance together anywhere." Not one to let barriers stop her, Mary flouted respectability and found "a girl in Ladies Hall who loved to dance as well as [she] did." They would sneak out together at night to boogie. Enjoying dancing might seem normal now in a post–*Dirty Dancing* world, but it was incredibly taboo at the time. Doing it and then daring to write about it was next-level. She wrote in her autobiography that they would "trip the light fantastic to our heart's content . . ."

Mary was a Black girl joy pioneer.

"IT WAS AGAINST THE RULES FOR GIRLS TO DANCE."

WHAT WILL I
BECOME?
WHAT WILL I
A Black
girl joy
pioneer
BECOME?
WHAT WILL I
BECOME?

MARY ELIZA CHURCH TERRELL was born in Memphis, Tennessee, in 1863, the same year President Abraham Lincoln signed the Emancipation Proclamation that changed the legal status under federal law of more than 3.5 million people from enslaved to free. "Mollie," as her family called her, was the daughter of two formerly enslaved people, and her upbringing was unique, especially for a Black woman raised during Reconstruction. Her family was both affluent and educated. Her dad, Robert Reed Church, went from being born enslaved to becoming one of the first millionaires in the South. Her mom, Louisa Ayers Church, developed a profitable chain of beauty parlors.

In 1866, the year after the Civil War ended, Mary was just three years old. A white mob shot her father during the Memphis Massacre and left him for dead. He survived, recovered, and resolved to stay in Memphis in spite of the anti-Black violence. While developing a business and real estate empire, he also heavily invested in the community, making philanthropy and charity for the Black community a priority.

Mary's parents thought the Memphis school system was inadequate and sent her to a boarding school in Yellow Springs, Ohio, at the age of six. She was the only Black girl at the school. She remained in Ohio for the entirety of her education, attending Antioch College laboratory school, Oberlin Academy, and then the prestigious Oberlin College. There she enrolled in the classical languages curriculum, which was intended for men, to the horror of her friends. They thought that learning Greek, a requirement in the course, "was unnecessary, if not positively unwomanly" and that knowing it "might ruin [her] chances of getting a husband." Mary wrote, "[They thought] I wouldn't be

The years following the Civil War were called the "Reconstruction era" because America had to rebuild a new society without the institution of slavery. Even after slavery ended, many still wanted to maintain the previous social order that had given them power over other people. Disgruntled white Southerners often violently lashed out at newly freed Black people. In 1866 in Memphis, white civilians and police killed forty-six Black people, many of whom were former Union soldiers, and injured many more. In what is now known as the Memphis Massacre or the Memphis riots, they burned houses, schools, and churches, decimating the Black community. The violent mobs wanted Black people to return to the plantations—or leave. Mary's father, Robert, defiantly refused to do either.

happy if I knew more than my husband, and they warned that trying to find a man in our group who knew Greek would be like hunting for a needle in a haystack." But Mary refused to shrink herself to make a man feel bigger.

Mary was an exceptional student and she established a reputation as a free thinker. She served as freshman class poet, joined Aelioian (a women's literary society), and edited the *Oberlin Review*. By the time she graduated, she was fluent in English, French, and German, and at Oberlin College she mastered Latin, and despite the warnings of becoming a spinster, Greek, too.

Like her parents, Mary believed in quality education for Black children. In 1887, after receiving her bachelors *and* masters degree before the age of twenty-five, Mary moved to Washington, DC. The nation's capital was the place to be for a woman of her experience, education, and ambition. She took a position teaching Latin at the M Street High School—the first African American public high school in the nation. The following year, she and her father sailed to the city of Berlin for the start of a two-year tour across the continent. Stops included London, Antwerp,

Brussels, Cologne, Frankfurt, Strasbourg, and Paris. Their expeditions involved carriage drives around major cities, steamer trips on scenic rivers, and train rides between destinations. Father and daughter enjoyed themselves immensely and it was with trepidation that Robert left Mary in Europe to study in France, Switzerland, and Germany when he had to return home.

While studying in Paris, Mary began keeping a diary (which she wrote in her *fifth* language, French). With repeated references to "R.H.T." she gives hints of her crush, Robert Heberton Terrell, a Harvard graduate who was a hotshot in DC's Black society. The two had met while working at M Street High School. On the diary pages, she ponders and dreams about her future: her penultimate French-language entry concludes with the question *Que deviendrai-je?* ("What will I become?") In 1890, she returned to the United States to find out the answer and what her future would hold.

Mary Church Terrell

LIFTING AS WE CLIMB, ONWARD AND UPWARD WE GO, STRUGGLING AND STRIVING AND HOPING.

Robert Heberton Terrell

Once again in DC, Mary started her transformation from teacher to activist, which would last for the next six decades. She attended her first suffrage convention in February 1891, the National Council of Women convention in Washington, DC. It wasn't easy to publicly stand for women's voting rights (literally): "[T]he presiding officer requested all those to rise who believed that women should have the franchise. Although the theater was well filled at the time, comparatively few rose . . . I forced myself to stand up." Mary explained, "In the early 1890's it required a great deal of courage for a woman publicly to acknowledge . . . she believed in suffrage for her sex when she knew the majority did not."

After attending a National American Woman Suffrage Association (NAWSA) convention in the early 1890s, she later recalled: "When the members of the Association were registering their protest against a certain injustice, I arose and said, 'As a colored woman, I hope this Association will include in the resolution the injustices of various kinds of which colored people are the victims.'" When Susan B. Anthony asked if Mary was a NAWSA member, she replied, "No, I am not . . . but I thought you might be willing to listen to a plea for justice by an outsider." Luckily Anthony was having a good day and invited Terrell to submit a resolution and "thus began a delightful, and helpful friendship."

The harmony didn't last, though. Eventually the two suffragists went from friends to frenemies when Susan B. narrowed NAWSA's focus from a broader women's rights platform to the sole goal of gaining women's suffrage, not fighting the racist restrictions on voting that oppressed Black women, like poll taxes and literacy tests. Susan B. Anthony and others thought this racist, narrow-minded approach to women's rights was a strategic way to encourage Southern white women to join the suffrage movement. But they refused to acknowledge the cost of their "strategy."

"She believed in suffrage for her sex when she knew the majority did not."

In the fall of 1891, true to her word that "under no circumstances would [she] marry a white man in the United States," Mary married her longtime crush, Robert Heberton Terrell, who was now a Harvard law graduate (and who, as predicted, it seems, did not speak Greek). Only twenty-eight, she was an older bride by the standards of her day, but the couple shared an egalitarian partnership matched in ambition and savvy. They raised two daughters: Phyllis, named after Phillis Wheatley, whose writing Mary loved and revered, and Mary's brother's daughter, whom the couple adopted.

THE FLASH POINT FOR the 1892 lynching of Thomas Moss started with a simple game of marbles. A team of Black boys and a team of white boys gathered near the Mississippi River, the lifeblood of Memphis, Tennessee. The Black kids won, and that sparked the trouble near People's Grocery Company at the corner of Mississippi Boulevard and Walker Avenue.

The children began fighting, and soon the adults were drawn in. There had been plenty of animosity in the neighborhood, which began brewing after eleven Black partners established the People's Grocery. A white grocer across the street, W. R. Barrett, was livid that this new enterprise was breaking up his monopoly.

Following the marbles skirmish, a threat was issued by the white adults that they would return Saturday night to clean out the People's Grocery. The store's owners armed themselves and waited inside. Around ten p.m., under the cover of darkness, a violent white crowd gathered and rushed through the back door. Three of the attackers were wounded. The Memphis newspaper carried headlines in their Sunday morning edition claiming the cops had been wounded just doing their jobs and called the People's Grocery "a low dive in which drinking and gambling were carried on" and "a resort of thieves and thugs." They rewrote the story entirely to place blame on the Black community.

As the backlash intensified, more than one hundred Black neighbors were dragged from their homes and jailed, including Thomas Moss, Calvin McDowell, and Will Stewart, who had been singled out as owners of the People's Grocery. A white mob rushed the jail on March 9, 1892, and removed the three men. Thomas reportedly begged for his life. His last words were, "Tell my people to go West—there is no justice for them here." The trio was then brutally murdered.

This terrible injustice sparked national outrage. Journalist Ida B. Wells was a dear friend of Thomas Moss and godmother to his daughter. His tragic death inspired her to launch her anti-lynching campaign. Mary was also a close childhood friend of Thomas Moss. Though she grew up with a life of relative privilege, the horror of the lynchings jarred her into committing all her efforts to civil and political rights.

THEY REWROTE THE STORY ENTIRELY TO PLACE BLAME ON THE BLACK COMMUNITY.

Ida B. Wells

Mississipp River

AFTER THE LYNCHING of her childhood friend in 1892, Mary Church Terrell founded the Colored Women's League of Washington, DC.

SHE SAW WOMEN'S SUFFRAGE AS ESSENTIAL TO ELEVATING THE STATUS OF BLACK WOMEN.

She was instrumental in the group's merge with the National Federation of Afro-American Women to form the National Association of Colored Women (NACW) in 1896. Ladies from both groups thought she was trustworthy, and Mary served two terms in office as the organization's president. Of the work the NACW was doing, she said, "Lifting as we climb, onward and upward we go, struggling and striving, and hoping . . . we look forward to a future large with promise and hope. Seeking no favors because of our color, nor patronage because of our needs, we knock at the bar of justice, asking an equal chance." Mary wasn't satisfied with opportunities for a privileged few; she wanted to lift up her entire community.

As NACW president and cofounder and a charter member of the National Association for the Advancement of Colored People (NAACP), Mary campaigned tirelessly with Black organizations and mainstream white organizations like Alice Paul's National Woman's Party (NWP). She saw women's suffrage as essential to elevating the status of Black women, and therefore, the entire race. She was an active suffragist constantly bringing the unique concerns of Black women to the table. In 1917, she and her teenage daughter Phyllis picketed the Wilson White House with Alice Paul and members of the NWP. Way before the term "intersectionality" was invented, Mary fought for suffrage and civil rights because she realized that both were inseparably intertwined in her identity and the intersecting forms of oppression all impacted her and other Black women.

After the Nineteenth Amendment was ratified in 1920, many Black women did vote, but others, particularly in the South, were denied their new constitutional rights. Representing the NAACP and the NACW, Mary and other Black suffragists wrote a resolution "urging Congress to appoint a committee to investigate the disfranchisement of colored women." Mary went directly to appeal to Alice Paul at the NWP headquarters with the other Black suffragists.

Despite the clarity of their request, Alice was incredulous, asking, "What do you women want me to do?" Mary explained that they wanted the white women to continue to pursue their own stated goal of *universal* suffrage: "I want you to tell us whether you endorse the enforcement of the 19th Amendment for *all* women," she said. Black women had worked and toiled for years to help achieve the national suffrage amendment and to their disgust, Alice refused to say she cared about suffrage for *all* women. Mary later reported her disappointment, writing, "Alice Paul had displayed the most painful lack of tact I had ever seen," and admitted that her feelings had been "lacerated" and her "heart so wounded" by racism, not only in daily life but also on the front lines of her work for equality.

In 1948, even though she had been treated poorly by her white colleagues in the struggle, Mary took the high road. She testified before Congress in favor of the NWP's Equal Rights Amendment, saying, "It is absolutely necessary for women to secure the rights for which they are asking so that they will no longer be the victims of the cruel injustice which will continue to humiliate, handicap and harass them in the future as it has done for so many years in the past." When she found out that a professional lobbyist for the National Negro Congress, a group formed in the 1930s to unite Black and white workers in the fight for racial justice, was lobbying *against* the ERA, she chastised her: "If negro women will study the Equal Rights Amendment and understand why it is needed and what it will do for them and for all women,

they cannot intelligently oppose it." Mary bemoaned, "It is humiliating to me to find that any of my people can be so misled on the question of equality."

Mary also went to bat for the National Woman's Party itself and countered the claims it was filled with only rich white society women. She refuted arguments that the amendment was against working people, saying, "The Equal Rights Amendment is not Anti-Labor, it is Anti-Unfair-Labor." Mary was willing to put differences aside for the common good, even after such disrespect by the white women behind the measure. She knew that the ERA stood to be a tool of liberation for *all* women, even if that wasn't why white ladies wanted it to succeed.

THE ERA STOOD TO BE A TOOL OF LIBERATION FOR ALL WOMEN.

EVER THE OPTIMIST, IN her late seventies, Mary Church Terrell returned to her love of dancing. She credited it for her longevity, saying, "There seems to be a sort of tradition that after a woman reaches a certain age she should not want to trip the light fantastic . . . I believe if a woman could dance or swim a half hour every day, her span of life would be greatly lengthened, her health materially improved, and the joy of living decidedly increased." Both dancing and political activism would bookend Mary's life.

For sixty years, she had lived in Washington, DC, which was a key civil rights battleground in 1950. On January 27 of that year, at Thompson's Restaurant, a cafeteria just a few blocks from the White House, the staff refused to serve Mary and her colleagues because three of them were "colored." She said, "It's my duty to send a message to the country, to the world that we are no longer patient with being pushed around." And at the age of eighty-seven, she launched an eight-week campaign to stop discrimination at stores and restaurants in the nation's capital.

Motivated by a desire for her country to measure up to its promises of equality and freedom, Mary said, "It pains me greatly to think that the capital of my own country, the Capital of the United States of America—is the only capital in the whole wide world in which restaurants refuse to serve colored people solely on account of their race." Throughout her life, she toured the globe, but had received some of the worst treatment at home. All these years later, after the lynching of her friend Thomas who ran the People's Grocery store, Black people were still not able to conduct business in peace, even in the epicenter of American democracy. Mary had once insisted on a certain level of propriety with her agitation, but later in life, she moved from proper to dignified, disgusted, and defiant. In addition to the picket lines, Mary's intention all along was to take her challenge to the courts.

Unlike many of the women in these pages, Mary Church Terrell *did* live to see the fruits of her fight. In 1953, after a years-long battle, the Supreme Court ruled in her favor to desegregate DC in a groundbreaking but now little-known case, *District of Columbia v. John R. Thompson Co., Inc.* When the *Afro-American*, a local Black newspaper, wrote about Mary's victory, its headline stated simply: EAT ANYWHERE. And Mary did. Within days, she returned to Thompson's, and they were forced to finally serve her. She said, "We went and we had a glorious time. I took a tray and got in line and received my food. When I got to the end of the line, a gentleman walked up to me, took my tray and escorted me to a table and asked me, 'Mrs. Terrell, is there anything else I can do for you?' And who do you think that man was? Why, it was the manager of the Thompson restaurants!" It was a sweet and savory victory.

Her triumph set a precedent for *Brown v. Board of Education*, the ruling that ended nationwide school segregation, just a year later. Mary lived to see the *Brown* decision come down from the Court, just two months before she died in 1954—a decision in favor of equality for which she personally paved the way.

EAT ANYWHERE

"IT'S MY DUTY TO SEND A MESSAGE TO THE COUNTRY, TO THE WORLD..."

ADELINA "NINA" OTERO-WARREN

Sufragista

Adelina "Nina" Otero-Warren was a prominent Latina suffragist who worked closely with the Congressional Union that Crystal Eastman (page 57), Lucy Burns (page 76), and Alice Paul (page 97) started. She was born in 1881 in New Mexico and spoke both English and Spanish fluently.

Like Mary Church Terrell, Nina worked to make the suffrage movement more inclusive. She insisted that the campaign for the vote include bilingual publications and speeches—many of which she translated and delivered herself. When Alice Paul asked Nina to take a leadership role in the national suffrage movement, she replied, "[I] will take a stand and a firm one whenever necessary for I am with you now and always."

Nina Otero-Warren was from a wealthy, well-connected family, and was at one point in her career the superintendent of the public schools in Santa Fe County. She used her political connections and leverage to forcefully lobby the state legislature to ratify the Nineteenth Amendment—which it did in February 1920. (That is only ten years after New Mexico officially became a state!) Her fight for inclusion included the hallways of her schools, too. As superintendent, Nina championed teaching Spanish as well as English in schools, and also wanted Native American students to learn about their languages and culture.

As soon as women were victorious in the suffrage amendment battle, Nina ran for Congress—the first-ever Latina to do so. She won the Republican nomination for a seat in the US House of Representatives, beating a man in the primary. But she lost the general election (by less than 9 percent) due to rumors about why her marriage to a man had ended after only two years. Although she had obtained a divorce, she continued to use her married name and told people that her husband had died (he had not) in order to escape the religious and social stigma of being divorced in old-timey Catholic country. The divorce cover-up cost her the congressional seat.

Turns out, Nina had left her husband for many reasons—including that she was a lesbian. She met her partner, Mamie Meadors, in 1922 when Mamie, a Protestant and a Texan (gasp!), joined as a volunteer for her congressional campaign. The two became inseparable and homesteaded a ranch together. They named their ranch "Las Dos" (meaning "Two Women"). Proving that a man is never necessary, they built three houses, a carriage house, a corral, and two rainwater cisterns together. They also fenced in 1,257 acres, in order to be granted land ownership in their own names. Mamie and Nina were together for over thirty years.

Adelina Otero-Warren

"I AM WITH YOU NOW AND ALWAYS."

ALICE PAUL

Like many of the strong women before her, Alice had an unquenchable thirst for learning and amassed degrees one after the other before the end of her career. In addition to her bachelor's degree in biology from Swarthmore, she earned a

"I never doubted that equal rights was the right direction. Most reforms, most problems are complicated. But to me there is nothing complicated about ordinary equality."

1885–1977

The young women were tired of the state-by-state ratification slog and wanted to solve the problem "a ed-up young feminists, including her one-time jail mate, and Eastman's college friend, Lucy Burns. "Th se they wouldn't have entrusted it to us young girls" She used the defeatist attitudes of the move

CHAPTER 7
ORDINARY EQUALITY

FED UP WITH BUSINESS as usual in the suffrage movement, Alice Paul was the one who recruited Crystal Eastman (page 57) to help convince the older NAWSA leaders to let them take a stab at the federal approach to suffrage. The young women were tired of the state-by-state ratification slog and wanted to solve the problem all at once. Alice had also recruited other fired-up young feminists, including her one-time jail mate and Crystal's college friend, Lucy Burns (page 76). The older women in the movement, including Susan B. Anthony and the new NAWSA President Carrie Chapman Catt, had all but given up on the nationwide solution. As Alice astutely observed, "They didn't take the work at all seriously, or else they wouldn't have entrusted it to us . . . young girls." She used the defeatist attitudes of the movement's stalwarts to her advantage to stage a suffrage coup—and it worked. Even Carrie, a powerful leader (and a lesbian!), eventually came around to the federal strategy and galvanized NAWSA's base to join up with the NWP. Harnassing the votes of women in the states that already had suffrage to pressure national leaders was part of her "Winning Plan."

During her life, Alice Paul was the bridge between the old and the new in many ways. She didn't start the movement for suffrage,

THE
BRIDGE
BETWEEN
THE OLD
AND THE
NEW IN
MANY WAYS

ORDINARY
EQUALITY
ORDINARY
EQUALITY
ORDINARY EQUALITY
ORDINARY EQUALITY

The party's **battle cry** became "Absolute equality!"

but she helped end it. In cementing the federal strategy as the collective goal, she pushed the Nineteenth Amendment over the finish line, introduced the ERA as a follow-up federal amendment, and then fought all the way through the 1970s women's liberation movement to get it ratified. She lived long enough to go full circle from a rabble-rousing upstart to a stick-in-the-mud that younger women rebelled against. Relentless and single-minded, she rode all the feminist waves. At times divisive, no matter how you come to view her, Alice Paul's impact on women's rights in this country, and the ERA specifically, are undeniable.

ALICE STOKES PAUL WAS born and raised on Paulsdale, the 173-acre farm her family owned in Mount Laurel Township, New Jersey. Her family followed the Hicksite Quaker faith, like many reformers of the day, including pioneering suffragist Lucretia Mott. Hicksites were much more progressive than other faith traditions of the time, encouraging women to speak for themselves (even publicly), but they hadn't completely eradicated female subordination. For example, women could be ministers but had to have separate-but-not-equal gender segregated meetings and were not the ultimate arbiters of decisions in homes or congregations. The Hicksites were also staunch abolitionists but did not allow Black people to join the faith. This belief in equality in theory, but not in practice (for everyone) would come to be reflected in many of Alice's decisions later in life.

However, Quakers did firmly believe in equal education for boys and girls, so Alice had the same opportunities to learn as her brothers. At fifteen, she was not only reading all the books available in her local library, but she was also attending local

Alice wanted to attend Princeton University in her home state of New Jersey, but Princeton didn't accept women. At the time she was denied entry, the school's president was Woodrow Wilson, who would later become president of the United States, and—spoiler alert—Alice would later become his worst nightmare.

suffrage meetings with her mom, Tacie Parry Paul. By age sixteen, she had been elected high school valedictorian. She then enrolled in Swarthmore College, a Quaker school cofounded by her grandfather and Lucretia Mott. (Later Alice would name the ERA the "Lucretia Mott Amendment" after her fellow Quaker agitator.) She chose to be a science major, even though fewer than 10 percent of women at the time did so, because it was the only subject she didn't already know anything about and she wanted to challenge herself. Alice's insistence that she could compete with any male peer on any subject often got her into trouble. Self-assured young women were apparently just as intimidating in 1901 as they are today.

Like many of the strong women before her, Alice had an unquenchable thirst for learning and amassed degrees one after the other. In addition to her bachelor's degree in biology from Swarthmore, she earned a master of arts degree in sociology from New York School of Philanthropy (now Columbia University), studied social work in England, and then came home to earn a PhD from the University of Pennsylvania. Later she would also earn not one but two different law degrees, an LLB (bachelor of laws), the precursor to the modern JD or juris doctor, from the Washington College of Law and a doctorate in civil law from American University.

In 1907, while studying in England, Alice caught her first glimpse of her future—in the form of British suffragist Christabel Pankhurst and her raucous suffragist meetings. Unlike the tame gatherings Alice had attended with her mother as a child, these British meetings were chaotic and loud. As Christabel spoke in favor of women's suffrage, the crowd shouted her down, blew horns, and made so much noise no one could hear her. Alice instinctively knew that if people were trying so hard to stop this woman from being heard, she must have had something vitally important to say. Alice remembered, "I thought, 'That's one group . . . I want to throw in all the strength I can give to help.'" Shortly thereafter, she joined in a suffrage demonstration. She wrote to her mother to inform her of her studies and tried to slyly slip in another update: "I have joined the 'suffragettes'—the militant party on the suffrage question." She didn't give any other details, but the idea of a "militant party" must have given her pacifist Quaker mom, Tacie, a heart attack.

Christabel Pankhurst and her mother, Emmeline Pankhurst, were radical British suffragists who were committed to their famous slogan "Deeds, not Words." They demanded action, not just talk from politicians, and they put their bodies on the line for suffrage. They led women to smash windows, fight back against cops, and destroy property through arson and explosions. The Pankhursts were often arrested for their "deeds" and staged hunger strikes in prison, where they were often force-fed. Alice Paul learned how to hunger strike and use other militant tactics from them.

In London, Alice marched in a huge pro-suffrage parade that was thirteen thousand marchers strong. In what could be considered a precursor to the Women's Marches of today, these women had built international solidarity between their movements, and there were delegations from many different countries. It was a dramatic event with women dressed in academic robes, costumes, and historic regalia, and ended in a huge rally. The seeds of what would become the 1913 American suffrage parade began to grow.

WELL-BEHAVED WOMEN SELDOM MAKE HISTORY.

Alice's experiences with the suffragists in England served as a crash course in militant protesting. She quickly learned that the suffrage women stuffed cotton under their clothes to serve as protective padding from the blows of the police, if things went awry. During her first arrest, police grabbed Alice so violently that the buttons of her coat popped off and her cotton padding spilled out. But thankfully the arrest was not all bad. A lifelong friendship was forged in the jailhouse when she struck up a conversation with Lucy Burns.

In 1909, Alice's protesting had garnered three arrests and one hunger strike in the span of one month. She had been arrested for smashing windows and screaming, "Votes for women! Votes for women!" at an event Winston Churchill was attending, and was sentenced to one month in prison. Her fearlessness caught the eyes of British suffrage leaders, who saw potential in Alice. It also caught the attention of the *New York Times*, landing her on the front page. When her mother was contacted for comment, she said in shock, "I cannot understand how all this came about. Alice is such a mild-mannered girl." But Alice had internalized what later became a popular feminist slogan—well-behaved women seldom make history.

DUE TO THE COVERAGE of her militant tactics, when Alice finished her social work studies and returned to the United States in 1909, she was already somewhat of a celebrity. The National American Woman Suffrage Association (NAWSA) that Susan B. Anthony had created by forcing two groups together was much more conservative than its British counterparts and, having not gained much traction, had all but given up on a federal suffrage amendment. NAWSA was committed to playing

Alice Paul

SHE DIDN'T START THE MOVEMENT FOR SUFFRAGE, BUT SHE HELPED END IT.

> The parade was an elaborate enactment of the history of women's achievement and the struggle for suffrage.

the state-by-state game, in part because they thought it was a way to make quicker gains. Of course, this approach also left a lot of women out of the equation, especially women of color in the South. Having the state grant suffrage was far less likely in places where the societal adherence to traditional attitudes about a "woman's place" was emphasized as a Southern value and because racist politicians limited voting access of Black men who would have otherwise been more sympathetic to the cause of suffrage for women and voted to give women suffrage.

Alice Paul, along with Crystal Eastman and Lucy Burns, convinced the NAWSA to let them take over federal action. In 1913, their first order of business was planning a gigantic parade—just like the one Alice had joined in London. She knew how to turn up the volume and bring the drama, so they chose the day before her old nemesis President Woodrow Wilson's inaugural parade to steal his thunder. The women felt this was a way to highlight that "one-half of the people have not participated in choosing the ruler who is being installed." The parade was an elaborate enactment of the history of women's achievement and the struggle for suffrage that, at that point, had already been going for sixty-five years.

The marchers were nervous that they would be attacked, and Washington's chief of police refused to provide them adequate protection. They were particularly on edge because President Wilson was from Virginia and droves of visitors were expected to arrive in DC from the South for the inauguration of who they saw as a white Southern son. Earlier on in the planning, Alice had encouraged Black women to march, even personally recruiting them. She felt compelled toward integration, telling a newspaper, "I am a Northern woman and . . . I belong to a Quaker family which has always taken a stand for the rights of the negro," but she caved to pressure from other organizers who insisted on a segregated march. Black women defied this order. Refusing to march at the back, Black suffrage leader Mary Church Terrell (page 79) marched with the integrated colleges delegation. Anti-lynching activist Ida B. Wells defied the segregation order and joined her fellow white suffragists from Illinois, integrating their delegation.

As the parade began, it became clear that racial integration was the least of their problems. Eight thousand women marched, but the throngs of men surrounding the parade route vastly out-numbered the marchers. The crowd started tearing down their banners, destroying their floats, and gearing up to physically attack them. A Connecticut suffragist yelled, "Girls, get out your hatpins; they are going to rush us!" These ladies weren't going down without a fight.

A melee ensued, with men assaulting women in the streets simply for exercising their right to free speech. It became a fortuitous disaster—and Alice couldn't have been more pleased. The brutal attacks against innocent women turned the tide

"GIRLS, GET OUT YOUR HATPINS; THEY ARE GOING TO RUSH US!"

"SILENT SENTINELS" OF LIBERTY.

Lucy Burns

Alice Paul

Crystal Eastman

Suffrage First

Vote Against Wil...
He Opposes National Woman Suff...
NATIONAL WOMAN'S PA...

of the public toward the cause of suffrage and put it, once again, on the front page of every newspaper. Their parade had worked; the flame of suffrage had all but gone out and the day's events had ignited it once again. Two weeks later, Alice took a delegation of women to the White House to nail down President Wilson's support (and probably to gloat over her success). He blew them off, but that was just the beginning of his dealings with Ms. Paul.

After President Wilson kept ignoring them, it was Harriot Eaton Stanton Blatch, the daughter of pioneering women's rights activist Elizabeth Cady Stanton, who first came up with the idea to picket the White House. The group was tired of being rebuffed. Harriot suggested they stand outside with signs as "silent sentinels" of liberty. And so they began daily vigils—rain, sleet, or snow—outside the White House gates. Never before in American history had the White House been a target of coordinated protests in this way.

Alice's mother again grew concerned about her daugher's tactics. Tacie had still not yet accepted that her daughter was the leader of a radical revolution. She registered her dissatisfaction: "I wish to make a protest against the methods you are adopting in annoying the President. . . . I hope thee will call it off." (Even revolutionaries have worried moms to contend with.)

And annoy the president, they did! It was right around the time they began burning a three-foot-tall paper effigy of President Wilson and copies of his speeches in a bonfire in front of the White House that the police began arresting the suffragists on trumped-up charges of blocking the traffic. Always thinking five steps ahead, Alice knew that the arrests would help garner public support as they had during her days in England. They

SUFFRAGISTS BURN WILSON IN EFFIGY

also helped build solidarity in the fractured suffrage movement, and NAWSA announced they would switch to putting all efforts into passing a federal amendment. Before they won the battle, over 2,000 National Woman's Party members had picketed the White House, more the 400 had been arrested, and 168 served serious jail time. They used the carceral system to their advantage, but they paid a high price.

Battle-worn from her time in the British women's suffrage movement, Alice Paul knew what it was like to starve herself as a form of political expression. She had been force-fed many times in jail and described the experience to her mother in a letter: "When it was over I was trembling from head to foot from shock, was covered with perspiration, felt sick at the stomach & my nose bled." She said it was excruciating and she never went through it without tears streaming down her face. So when she asked women to be ready for incarceration for picketing President Wilson at the White House, she understood precisely what she was asking of them, and it was nothing she wasn't willing to suffer herself.

ON JUNE 4, 1919, Congress passed the Susan B. Anthony amendment—now the Nineteenth Amendment—over forty years after it was first introduced. Later that day, fellow suffragists found Alice Paul not celebrating their victory but at her desk. She'd immediately started in on the next project, telling reporters there was more to do. "Popular opinion believes that the discriminations against women will be brushed aside with the ratification of the Nineteenth Amendment. But this is not true," said Alice, who explained that women had to conduct an ongoing campaign against injustices. Although Alice did not take a break to mark the occasion, one surprising person did—her mom. After all the grief she had given her daughter, Tacie Paul memorialized the event in the family scrapbook, writing, "Alice at last saw her dream realized."

Because there's no rest for the weary, in early 1921, the NWP members met in Washington to regroup and settle on their

Alice ended up in jail many times. On on occasion, she heard a chorus of women's voices outside her cell window. She looked out to see ninety NWP members standing below shouting, "West Virginia greets you," "Oklahoma is with you," and "New York salutes you." They urged her to hold on. Senator Andrieus Jones, chairman of the Committee on Woman Suffrage, went to visit suffragists in jail to investigate the horrifying conditions. Shaken by what he saw, he immediately told his committee to take favorable action on the suffrage bill, and that got the ball rolling in Congress. It worked!

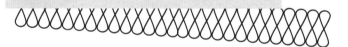

The NWP had an epic index card system, akin to an elaborate modern-day Google spreadsheet, that was created to track every member of Congress. The group's lobbying efforts often involved using the index system to track and do outreach to the secretaries of elected officials in order to get their support. One NWP member said, "This is the way women worked, they could always find a back door to get in . . . You see, we had women in every department in Washington."

next campaign. They agreed in advance to concentrate on equal rights for women and the removal of all laws that discriminated against them. Alice was laser-focused, as always. Crystal Eastman said of her, "Alice Paul is a leader of action, not of thoughts. She is a general, a supreme tactician." She wanted the NWP to act on just one common goal, and the party's battle cry became "Absolute equality!"

But not everyone could agree on a definition of "absolute." A group of Black women from fourteen different states met with Alice and told her that after the Nineteenth Amendment was ratified, they had tried to vote in the 1920 election but had been thwarted by racist laws already in place to keep Black men (and therefore Black women) from the polls. Mary Church Terrell told Alice she wanted "to see that no colored women were disbarred from voting on account of their race." The Black suffragists wanted the NWP to keep fighting for suffrage until all women could vote. But just as she had with the 1913 parade, Alice declined to stand up for racial justice.

The National Woman's Party moved on to their next project. They knew in order to make any progress "you must change the basis . . . of our whole legal system; and you can only do it . . . from the very top, which is the Constitution." Alice enrolled in law school so that no one arguing against her would know any more than she did. She chose Washington College of Law, a school founded by Emma Gillett, a fellow suffragist and NAWSA's treasurer who had supported Alice against the old-guard suffragists who disapproved of her radical tactics.

Alice drafted the Equal Rights Amendment in consultation with many other women who had been part of the movement, as well as some male ally attorneys. It was initially intended to be a "Woman's Bill of Rights" that would ensure full citizenship following the ratification of the Nineteenth Amendment, and included nine different sections. After three years of intense discussion and drafting, they chose to present their shiny new amendment. It was unveiled in 1923 at the 75th anniversary celebration of the first women's rights convention in Seneca Falls, New York, since Alice was a genius at garnering media attention with pageantry. Alice pointed out what she had learned from the suffrage fight—that if they had to do a laborious state-by-state campaign to change all the sexist laws one by one, they'd make very little progress even by its 150th anniversary. Once again, Alice Paul was right.

The ERA's language was simple: "Men and women shall have equal rights throughout the United States and every place subject to its jurisdiction. Congress shall have the power to enforce this article by appropriate legislation." The amendment was first introduced in Congress in 1923, sponsored in the House of Representatives by Daniel Anthony of Kansas, the nephew of suffragist leader Susan B. Anthony. He said he proudly supported the amendment because it would "establish what I have been

THE ERA'S LANGUAGE WAS SIMPLE: "MEN AND WOMEN SHALL HAVE EQUAL RIGHTS."

In 1932, after she became the first woman to fly alone across the Atlantic, aviator Amelia Earhart joined the NWP delegation to lobby Herbert Hoover for the ERA. She said, "In aviation the Department of Commerce recognizes no legal differences between men and women licensed to fly. I feel that similar equality should be carried into all fields of endeavor."

brought up to feel a democracy should establish—equality for men and women in all fields."

The most vehement ERA opposition came from labor groups who feared it would be used to invalidate the protective laws for female workers they had fought so hard for. Former allies like the social reformer Jane Addams turned against Alice. Florence Kelley, once her friend, now called her a "fiend." Even with this energized opposition, Alice's relentless determination helped gather steam and supporters for the amendment.

Things dragged along in the 1940s and '50s. There was a lot of backlash against women after WWII. A special issue of *Life* magazine in 1956 focused on the problems of American women—suggesting that their difficulties were the result of a "preoccupation with rights." (Eye roll.) Seeking other avenues for advocacy, Alice worked on international equality. In 1938, she founded a World Woman's Party that operated until 1958. She fought Eleanor Roosevelt, who didn't want to muddy the waters with gender issues, to get women's rights included in the United Nations' Universal Declaration of Human Rights. Alice prevailed, and the words "equal rights of men and women" were included in the final draft of the declaration. Her imprint was international in scope.

ALICE PAUL NEVER MARRIED or had children—the ERA was her baby. She put all her time and energy into working on pieces of the policy puzzle, and chipping away at inequality. Under her leadership, the NWP would go on to draft six hundred pieces of legislation over the years, over half of which became law.

Never afraid to make dubious alliances to further her causes, in 1963 Alice contacted Representative Howard W. Smith. He was a racist congressman from Virginia who had sponsored the ERA in the House in the 1940s but did not support the civil rights movement. Alice convinced him to introduce an amendment to Title VII that would prohibit gender discrimination in the workplace in addition to "race, color, religion, or national origin." Smith thought the "sex amendment" would help kill the bill and basically introduced it on a lark, playing it up for laughs when he spoke about it on the floor. Many leaders of the civil rights movement were furious about the amendment because, ironically, they they agreed with Smith's hypothesis that it would sink the whole bill (which really tells you something about the state of women's rights at the time). But the "sex amendment" to the bill passed 168 to 133, and in 1964 the Civil Rights Act was signed into law with the word crucial to women—"sex"—still in it. Gambling with women's rights in order to protect racism backfired on Representative Smith, and we ended up with measures to protect against both.

In 1966, the National Organization for Women (NOW) was created one evening in feminist author Betty Friedan's hotel room

One of the cofounders of NOW was a woman named Aileen Hernandez, a Black civil rights and labor organizer. She became the organization's second president from 1970 to 1971, key years for the ERA.

In February 1970, twenty NOW leaders disrupted hearings of the US Senate Subcommittee on the Constitution, demanding that the ERA be considered by the full Congress. When a hearing was finally granted, Aileen testified in support of the amendment. She said: "Gentlemen, women are enraged. We are dedicated, and we mean to become first-class citizens in this country."

in Washington, DC. When NOW invited Alice Paul to join, she accepted and immediately set about convincing them to adopt the ERA as their legislative agenda. NWP members infiltrated the new group and got them jazzed about the amendment. At its second national conference in 1967, NOW voted to make the passage of the ERA one of its goals. As a result, in the 1960s and '70s, it was the younger, more savvy group NOW, not Alice Paul's outdated NWP, that led the campaign for passage of the ERA.

Alice was the only suffrage leader of her time who lived to witness the resurgence of the movement. With the momentum of the second-wave feminist movement now behind it, the ERA finally passed in Congress by 354 to 24 in the House and 84 to 8 in the Senate in October 1971, far more than the two-thirds required by the Constitution. The ERA appeared to be on fire, but when an excited group of young women rushed to the NWP headquarters to find Alice after the ERA passed, they found her, as always, at her desk. This time she wasn't working, she was weeping—and not tears of joy. She feared that the seven-year time limit Congress had attached to the proposing clause of the amendment when they passed it would eventually kill it. Alice also feared that because the language "several states" had been removed from the amendment text approved by Congress, states' rights arguments would be used to kill it during the ratification process. The young feminists thought she was crazy to be so apprehensive.

The ERA had huge momentum behind it and was on the national platform of both the Democratic and Republican parties. It was immediately ratified by 22 of the necessary 38 states that first year. Everyone thought Alice's concerns had been overblown. But in the end, her prophetic vision was spot-on, and she died in 1977 with the amendment still unratified. Having been so successful in getting one constitutional amendment ratified in her early thirties, she was never able to see her dreams of full constitutional equality realized. ✗

Everyone thought Alice's concerns had been overblown. But in the end, her prophetic vision was spot-on.

Alice Paul

Mahatma Gandhi

DEEDS ARE BETTER THAN WORDS.

MAHATMA GANDHI
The Birth of nonviolent Struggle

Indian leader Mohandas Karamchand Gandhi was visiting London in 1906 and 1909 and witnessed firsthand the kinds of dramatic suffrage actions Alice Paul had taken part in. In an article in his journal *Indian Opinion*, Gandhi wrote of the British suffragists: "Today the whole country is laughing at them, and they have only a few people on their side. But undaunted, these women work on steadfast in their cause. They are bound to succeed and gain the franchise, for the simple reason that deeds are better than words."

"The brave women of England are continuing their campaign. Their courage and their capacity for suffering are inexhaustible," he wrote. Gandhi's future bold, nonviolent actions were inspired by the daring campaigns of the suffragists. He noted that there was "much to learn" from the women fighting for the vote and said their willingness to suffer, be imprisoned, or even die for their cause made them a "soul force." In 1913, motivated by the actions of the suffragists he had encountered in England, Gandhi ate only one meal a day for twenty weeks, and he encouraged his followers to do the same. His fasting tactics escalated as his campaign for independence continued, and his protests eventually helped drive the British out of India.

These movements for justice spanned time and geography, and decades later in the United States—inspired by Gandhi, who had in turn been inspired by the suffragists—civil rights activists like Martin Luther King Jr. began using Gandhi's tactics of nonviolent direct action. But many of these tactics were originally developed and practiced by women who were seeking equality at the ballot box.

PAULI MURRAY

1910–1985

"I want to see America be what she says she is and I consider it part of my responsibility to do that."

Race was just one of the ways Pauli felt as were living in-between. Even from a very age Pauli hated to wear dresses, so Aunt permitted pants and called Pauli her "litt

CHAPTER 8

JANE CROW

LONG BEFORE KIMBERLÉ CRENSHAW coined the term "intersectionality," Pauli Murray insisted on the indivisibility of their identity as a Black person and a woman. S/he explained that s/he came to every problem as the sum of all their parts: "And since as a human being I cannot allow myself to be fragmented into a Negro at one time, a woman at another, or a worker at another, I must find a unifying principle in all these movements to which I can adhere. . . . This, it seems to me, is not only good politics but may be the price of survival."

All the things that hindered Pauli's growth from birth—race, gender, class—were used by others to deem Pauli unworthy, but s/he found pride in heritage, authenticity, and hard work. Pauli's lifelong quest was to demand entrance to institutions previously closed to those s/he called the

A note on language choice and pronouns: Born Anna Pauline Murray in 1910, Pauli often chose not to use that given name and wrestled with issues of gender identity throughout life. Pauli regulary dressed and presented as male, particularly when younger, and attempted for decades to get hormone replacement therapy from medical professionals. Given ample evidence of a trans or nonbinary experience, Pauli has posthumously been identified by many as transgender. Pauli consistently indicated feeling "incompletely female," and actively used the phrase "he/she personality." In this chapter, I follow the lead of the Pauli Murray Center for History and Social Justice and use s/he and they/them pronouns when discussing Pauli's early life and she/her/hers when discussing Pauli's later years, after the founding of the National Organization for Women. This is an attempt to follow Pauli's expressed preferences, honor their status as a transgender pioneer, and avoid misgendering a person who contributed so much to the cause of gender equality. I hope this will help you, dear reader, embrace the magnificent journey of Pauli's life with an open heart.

LIVING IN-BETWEEN
BETWEEN
LIVING IN-
BETWEEN
LIVING IN-BETWEEN

"I only know how I feel and what makes me happy."

"minority of minorities." Pauli's persistence almost always paid off, and if it didn't, the other side lived to regret it.

Pauli said, "As one begins to assume that one is equal to other people, not superior or inferior, but equal, as a human being . . . one does begin to feel free."

———————

PAULI WAS BORN IN 1910 in Baltimore, Maryland, to Agnes Fitzgerald and William Murray. After Agnes died when Pauli was just four years old, s/he was sent to live with their namesake, Aunt Pauline Fitzgerald Dame, and grandparents Robert George and Cornelia Smith Fitzgerald, in Durham, North Carolina. Pauli's father, a graduate of Howard University who became a teacher and later a principal in the Baltimore public school system, suffered from mental illness and was unable to care for his children. He was eventually confined to the Hospital for the Negro Insane, and after moving to North Carolina, Pauli saw him alive only one more time, when Aunt Pauline took Pauli to visit him. The next time Pauli saw him, he was in a coffin at his funeral—he had been murdered by a racist guard at the hospital, the victim of a hate crime. Pauli was just thirteen when he died, and later wrote, "The most significant fact of my childhood was that I was an orphan."

This could have been one of the reasons Pauli struggled with a sense of belonging and identity. S/he wrote about being biracial, "being neither very dark nor very fair" and "without identity," saying, "In a world of black-white opposites, I had no place." Race was just one of the ways Pauli felt as if s/he were living in-between. Even from a very young age Pauli hated to wear dresses, so Aunt Pauline permitted pants and called Pauli her

At age ten, Pauli started a Memorial Day tradition of planting a US flag on grandfather Robert's gravesite. He'd fought in the Civil War as a Union soldier and risked his life to end slavery. The flag Pauli planted was a small act of defiance because it was the only American flag waving amid a sea of Confederate flags. In Pauli's memoir, called *Proud Shoes*, s/he said the flag "bore mute testimony to the irrefutable fact that I was an American. Whatever else they denied me, they could not take from me this right and the undiminished stature it gave me. For there at least at Grandfather's grave with the American flag in my hands, I could stand very tall and in proud shoes."

"little boy-girl." Pauli attempted to push back against suffocating norms whenever possible and favored stereotypically boy's chores and pastimes. S/he refused to learn to cook (and never did!). Pauli later wrote to Aunt Pauline, "this little 'boy-girl' personality as you jokingly call it sometimes gets me into trouble . . . the world does not accept my pattern of life. And to try to live by society's standards always causes me such inner conflict that at times it's almost unbearable. I don't know whether I'm right or whether society (or some medical authority) is right—I only know how I feel and what makes me happy." Pauli's constant need to push against boundaries as a young person helped form a resolve to eliminate them later in life.

Multiple emotional breakdowns landed Pauli in hospitals for psychological care. Early on, each time s/he pressed the medical staff to investigate whether s/he had hidden male sex organs. It was Pauli's theory that s/he was intersex and that was why s/he felt so masculine and attracted to women yet not at all like a lesbian. A later surgery proved this theory not to be true, but Pauli went on to struggle with the question of gender identity throughout life. There was no public or scientific discourse at the time

Pauli Murray

"AS ONE BEGINS TO ASSUME THAT ONE IS EQUAL TO OTHER PEOPLE, NOT SUPERIOR OR INFERIOR, BUT EQUAL, AS A HUMAN BEING...

ONE DOES BEGIN TO FEEL FREE."

Pauli defied arbitrary categorization in all aspects of life. Though as a child s/he couldn't avoid segregated schools, Pauli tried to avoid segregation whenever possible. Young Pauli refused to get on Jim Crow streetcars, opting instead to walk or ride a bike. Pauli also refused to go to the movies because the cinemas were segregated, and instead chose to read voraciously. Anything Pauli could do to opt out of segregation, they did. It was a personal protest against injustice.

about what it meant to be transgender—in fact, there wasn't even a term for it. Pauli was so ahead of their time, it was like trying to describe an internal, personal experience no one even had words for yet.

Even with such an excruciatingly difficult childhood, Pauli graduated from Hillside High School in 1926 at age fifteen as the number one student. The yearbook showed a photo of a confident young person, hair in a bob, with the name "Paul." S/he experimented with many names including "Pete" (short for Peter Pan), "Dude," and "Paul." Later they settled on "Pauli," and offered this motto in the yearbook: "The best I can do to help others is to be the best I can myself."

Having visited there once growing up, Pauli idolized New York City, where s/he saw Black people live and move more freely than in the South. So Pauli headed north at the first opportunity after graduation. After one additional year of high school in New York to qualify for admission, Pauli attended Hunter College and financed their university studies with a myriad of odd jobs. New York provided a new, rich cultural experience, and in Harlem, Pauli was inspired by performances, literature, and lectures by women like Mary Church Terrell (page 79) and Mary McLeod Bethune about the contributions of Black women in America.

After graduating college (1 of 4 Black students in a class of 247), Pauli fell in love with a woman named Peggie Holmes. The two were inseparable, and would take long road trips together, hitch-hiking all around the country. Pauli described the conundrum, "falling in love with a member of my sex . . . finding no opportu-nity to express such an attraction in normal ways—sex life, marriage, dating." Peggie loved Pauli, but ultimately she could not accept Pauli as a partner or enter a permanent romantic coupling, and Pauli suffered a heartbreaking emotional collapse when they broke up in 1937.

In 1938, Pauli began an ultimately unsuccessful campaign to enter graduate school at the University of North Carolina (UNC). Pauli's white ancestors had donated much of their vast estate and family fortune to the university, which had a policy of admitting only white students. But despite the family contri-bution and the fact that Pauli's great-great grandfather had been a UNC trustee, s/he received this gut punch of a letter from the Dean: "Under the laws of North Carolina, and under the resolutions of the Board of Trustees of the University of North Carolina, members of your race are not admitted to the university."

Pauli met with Thurgood Marshall of the National Association for the Advancement of Colored People (NAACP)—the civil rights organization Mary Church Terrell had helped found. It's unclear why the NAACP decided not to take up Pauli's case, though it may have had something to do with perceived sexual orientation and Pauli's ability to be a "desirable plaintiff." ("Respectability" was a big concern in the civil rights movement at the time.)

"The best I can do to help others is to be the best I can myself."

"MY PROBLEM ISN'T MINE ALONE, IT IS THE PROBLEM OF MY PEOPLE."

But despite the lack of support from the NAACP, Pauli managed to drum up national publicity. Pauli wrote to first lady Eleanor Roosevelt in hopes that the enclosed letter to her husband would have a better chance of actually reaching him. Pauli wrote, "I know he has the problems of our nation on his hands, and I would not bother to write him, except that my problem isn't mine alone, it is the problem of my people, and in these trying days, it will not let me or any other thinking negro rest. Need I say more?"

Pauli reminded Mrs. Roosevelt that they had met once in person when the first lady visited Camp TERA (Temporary Emergency Relief Assistance), a camp for thousands of unemployed women that the federal government set up for recreation and conservation projects during the Great Depression, which Pauli had attended. Perhaps because of this personal connection, and to Pauli's surprise, Mrs. Roosevelt wrote back, though she cautioned that "great change comes slowly" and not to "push too fast."

This was the inauspicious start of an unlikely friendship between Pauli and Mrs. Roosevelt, one that was filled with support but also candor. They exchanged hundreds of letters over their lifetimes, some filled with mutual admiration. "If ever there were a Woman's Revolution, I'm afraid you'd have to run for President," Pauli told Eleanor. But in other letters, Pauli was blunt and full of outrage at the injustices perpetrated against vulnerable people in this country. Pauli's directness never hindered their friendship and s/he visited Mrs. Roosevelt many times, including for personal visits at the White House with Aunt Pauline in tow.

In March 1940, Pauli was arrested and imprisoned for refusing to sit at the back of a bus in Richmond, Virginia, on a trip down South with a friend. Before s/he was arrested, Pauli wrote all their personal information down and handed it to another Black passenger, asking him to tell Aunt Pauline to contact the NAACP. This time, the NAACP did agree to help, and Pauli was released. Not yet done with Virginia, Pauli got a job with the Workers Defense League trying to save the life of a Black sharecropper, Odell Waller, who was convicted of murdering a white farmer. Odell claimed it was self-defense, and Pauli lead a two-year campaign to save his life, officially launching a career as a civil rights activist.

In 1941, Pauli enrolled at Howard University with the intention of becoming a civil rights lawyer. S/he was one of only two female-presenting students to enroll, and the only one to complete the first year. On Pauli's first day of classes at Howard Law, a professor announced that he didn't know why women even went to law school. As the male students laughed, Pauli responded with a silent vow: "The professor didn't know it, but he had just guaranteed that I would be the top student in his class." While no stranger to racial discrimination, law school is where Pauli said, "[I] first became conscious of the twin evil of discriminatory sex bias, which I quickly labeled Jane Crow."

Even the professor Pauli had met while working on Odell Waller's case, who gave

Camp TERA and other similar facilities set up for women were dubbed "She–She–She" camps playing on the abbreviation CCC for the men's Civilian Conservation Corps camps. Eleanor Roosevelt was a supporter and benefactor of the camps and said, "As a group women have been neglected in comparison with others, and throughout this depression have had the hardest time of all."

At Howard, Pauli took a civil rights seminar. Other students laughed when s/he argued the Fourteenth Amendment's equal protection clause should be used to overturn *Plessy v. Ferguson*, the Supreme Court case that upheld state-mandated segregation laws. Pauli bet a skeptical professor, Spottswood Robinson, ten dollars that *Plessy* would be overturned within the next twenty-five years, and their last paper for Howard Law proposed a way to use the Thirteenth and Fourteenth Amendments to do so. Professor Robinson kept Pauli's paper and referred to it a decade later when he and the NAACP attorneys were preparing *Brown v. Board of Education*, though Pauli was never publicly credited with the idea or the victory. (Sheesh! Robinson should have at least given Pauli the ten bucks he owed!)

the encouragement to attend law school by saying Pauli had "what it takes to be a good lawyer," accepted their exclusion from an event for men. Pauli said, "the discovery that . . . men I deeply admired because of their dedication to civil rights, men who themselves had suffered racial indignities, could countenance exclusion of women from their professional association aroused an incipient feminism in me long before I knew the meaning of the term . . . I had entered law school preoccupied with the racial struggle and single-mindedly bent upon becoming a civil rights attorney, but I graduated an unabashed feminist as well."

PAULI GRADUATED AS THE valedictorian of the Howard Law class of 1944. Eleanor Roosevelt sent Pauli a bouquet of posies and a card from the president for graduation. Pauli had come a long way and had bested all the self-righteous male students—a lot to be proud of.

Typically each year Harvard Law accepted the Howard valedictorian for advanced studies. One of Pauli's former classmates, whom s/he had outdone several times in class, was already studying there. Alas, Pauli received a rejection similar to the earlier one from UNC—only this time on the grounds of gender, not race. The Harvard admissions committee told Pauli, "Your picture and the salutation on your college transcript indicate that you are not of the sex entitled to be admitted to Harvard Law School." Pauli quickly retorted, "Gentlemen, I would gladly change my sex to meet your requirements, but since the way to such change has not been revealed to me, I have no recourse but

"I HAD ENTERED LAW SCHOOL PREOCCUPIED WITH... BECOMING A CIVIL RIGHTS ATTORNEY, BUT I GRADUATED AN UNABASHED FEMINIST AS WELL."

In 19__ _____ _____ _____ _____ _____ _____ _____ _____ _____ _____ _____ _____ _____ _____ ention of becoming a civil _____ _____ _____ _____ ny two female students to enroll, and the only one _____ _____ _____ e the first year. On Pauli's first day of classes at Howard Law, a professor announced that he didn't know why women even went to law school. As the male students laughed, Pauli responded with a silent vow: "The pr__ _____ _____ _____ _____ _____ but he had just guaranteed that I would be the top student__ _____ _____ _____ _____ stranger to racial discrimination, law school is where Pa__ _____ _____ _____ _____ conscious of the twin evil of discriminatory sex bias, ___ _____ _____ _____ Crow."

In 1960, Pauli traveled to Ghana to teach law. Upon returning, Pauli enrolled at Yale Law School (in your face, Harvard!), studying for an advanced law degree in addition to mentoring several young women activists, including Marian Wright Edelman, Eleanor Holmes Norton (future fighter for the ERA!), and Patricia Roberts Harris, who all became leaders in their own right. Pauli treated mentoring young women as an important duty.

to appeal to you to change your minds on this subject. Are you to tell me that one is as difficult as the other?" Touché.

In the intervening years, Pauli took up the pen to chronicle the injustices s/he had faced, and in 1956, *Proud Shoes: The Story of an American Family*, an autobiography of how white supremacy and anti-Blackness impacted Pauli's family, was published. After its release, Pauli was offered a job in the litigation department at the New York law firm Paul, Weiss, Rifkind, Wharton & Garrison. While working there, Pauli met Irene Barlow, the firm's office manager, and sparks began to fly. Even though they had a seventeen-year romantic relationship, little is known about the details because Pauli, someone who normally saved every scrap of paper, destroyed all of Irene's letters later in life, perhaps to protect their privacy. What we do know is that they were a dedicated and loving couple all those years.

DURING THE EARLY 1960s, Pauli worked closely with Bayard Rustin, Martin Luther King Jr., and many other civil rights leaders, and was increasingly bothered by sexism present in the movement. In August 1963, Pauli wrote to

Philip Randolph, whom s/he had known from Howard, asserting s/he was "increasingly perturbed over the blatant disparity between the major role which Negro women have played and are playing in the crucial grass-roots levels of our struggle and the minor role of leadership they have been assigned in the national policy-making decisions."

Pauli was among the 250,000 demonstrators who participated in the historic March on Washington for Jobs and Freedom on August 28, 1963. But the march's leaders had refused to permit any women to speak at the Lincoln Memorial because, they argued, there was already one on the program. (Turns out she was a singer, not a speaker.) Pauli said, "it was bitterly humiliating for Negro women on August 28 to see themselves accorded little more than token recognition in the historic March on Washington." Pauli was fed up with male organizers.

By 1966 Pauli had completely had it with men, and dove into organizing with more women. At the third-annual Conference of State Commissions on the Status of Women in Washington, DC, Pauli and Betty Friedan, feminist author of the *Feminine Mystique* and a leading figure in the women's movement, discussed forming a group to increase momentum for women's equality. Pauli said they needed an "NAACP for women." Friedan invited fifteen women to her hotel room in DC and together they launched the National Organization for Women. On a hotel napkin, Friedan scribbled the purpose of the new group: "to take the actions needed to bring women into the mainstream of American society now . . . in fully equal partnership with men." The next tidal wave of feminism was about to come crashing down on Washington.

One of the things Pauli fought for, like Alice Paul and others, was the inclusion of a "sex amendment" into the Civil Rights Act. She

"It was bitterly humiliating for Negro women . . . to see themselves accorded little more than token recognition in the historic March on Washington."

Pauli and longtime friend and civil rights coconspirator Dorothy Kenyon combined forces to convince the ACLU board to drop its decades-long opposition to the ERA. After receiving their materials for a planned meeting to debate the ERA, they sent a telegram to the entire board: "Board materials include paper on Equal Rights Amendment written by four men law professors and (inadvertently) not one syllable from any women. We are aghast at such gallant effrontery. Hell hath no rage greater than a woman scorned. Beware of more materials." Not long after that doozy of a telegram, the ACLU reversed their position and endorsed the ERA.

was one of the few civil rights activists excited about the addition of the word "sex" to the bill. She said, "I was overjoyed to learn of the House action, particularly because, as a Negro woman, I knew that in many instances it was difficult to determine whether I was being discriminated against because of race or sex." Pauli pitched in to help keep the "sex amendment" to Title VII when it went over to the Senate side for approval. And, as we've learned, they were successful. A huge victory for women!

Pauli was invited by President John F. Kennedy to sit on the Committee on Civil and Political Rights as a part of his President's Commission on the Status of Women via its chair (and Pauli's old friend), Eleanor Roosevelt. When asked to write a memorandum for the commission on women's constitutional rights and the feasibility of an amendment, Pauli suggested a route to gender equality through the Fourteenth Amendment, hoping it would make the ERA unnecessary since a constitutional amendment is so incredibly hard to pass and ratify. As a result, the commission declined to endorse the ERA. But then Eleanor Roosevelt, who had long vociferously opposed the ERA on labor grounds, died in 1962.

Losing Mrs. Roosevelt's opposition, combined with the subpar success of Pauli's proposed judicial approach of wiggling women into the Constitution under the Fourteenth Amendment (à la RBG-style litigation), helped change Pauli's mind to become a public supporter of the Equal Rights Amendment. Having had a change of heart, Pauli testified at a 1970 ERA Senate hearing in favor of ratification of the ERA, saying, "I suggest that what the opponents of the Amendment most fear is not equal rights but equal power and responsibility."

There were longstanding ideas in many corners of society that the ERA was a wealthy white women's issue. But Pauli disagreed, saying, "Negro women as a group have the most to gain from the adoption of the Equal Rights Amendment . . . [T]he Equal Rights Amendment strikes a blow at the powerlessness which all women share, but which Negro women experience in intensified form." She wrote that the "protections" so many opponents were afraid of losing had never applied to Black women. "Negro women enjoy neither the

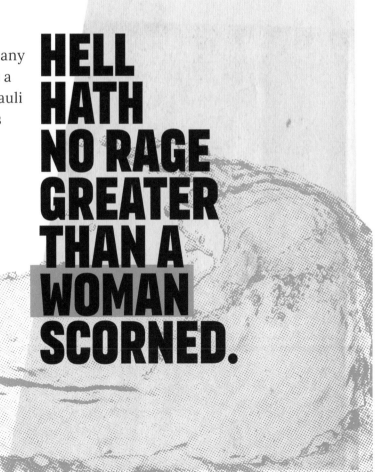

HELL HATH NO RAGE GREATER THAN A WOMAN SCORNED.

When Pauli was in the hospital at the end of her life, she had a sign posted over the bed that read, "Please refer to this patient as the Reverend Dr. Pauli Murray." In 2012, Pauli was posthumously named to Episcopal sainthood. So now she's literally a saint. Pauli is buried under the same headstone as her partner, Irene Barlow, in Cypress Hills Cemetery in Brooklyn, New York.

advantages of the idealizations of 'womanhood' and 'motherhood' which are part of American mythology, nor the 'protections' extended to women which opponents of the Equal Rights Amendment are so zealous to preserve." Black women stood to gain only from a formalization of constitutional rights.

IN 1973, FOLLOWING THE death of Pauli's partner, Irene, she left a tenured position at Brandeis University to become a candidate for ordination at the General Theological Seminary. Pauli wanted to jump over one final hurdle people thought was impossible. It baffled friends and family, but was a classic Pauli move: to train for a position that wasn't available. When she entered the seminary, Episcopalians still did not even ordain women (and certainly not gender-nonconforming people).

Among the many issues she cared about, Pauli Murray fought for ecclesiastical equality. "Church politics," Pauli wrote, "is probably the ultimate politics." The Episcopal Church reversed course while she was studying and Pauli was recognized as the first African American woman ever vested as an Episcopal priest—and though not recognized as such at the time, likely the first ordained person of trans experience. After ordination, Pauli was among the clergy who participated in the funeral services for Alice Paul, coauthor and ultimate champion of the ERA.

Historical justice was served when, despite Pauli having such trouble getting admitted to universities, one of the residential colleges at Yale was named in her honor. The sweetest victory of all, though, was when the University of North Carolina, which had denied Pauli admission because she was Black, renamed its Hamilton Hall—named after an unabashed white supremacist— to Pauli Murray Hall to honor Pauli's legacy.

RUTH BADER GINSBURG

Lifelong ERA Advocate

Pauli's prescient legal strategy of using the Fourteenth Amendment to insert women into the Constitution was used by a young lawyer named Ruth Bader Ginsburg in the 1971 case *Reed v. Reed*, where in a unanimous decision, the Supreme Court held that an Idaho law's dissimilar treatment of men and women was unconstitutional. This time, Pauli was credited for being the genius behind the legal strategy—by the "Notorious RBG" herself on the cover of the court brief. This litigation method was used to make great strides for women but was never able to get as high a level of judicial scrutiny for women as the court uses for other protected categories (like race, religion, and national origin).

In 1973, RBG wrote a law review article titled, "The Need for the Equal Rights Amendment." In 1978 she wrote a piece in the *Harvard Women's Law Journal* called, "The Equal Rights Amendment Is the Way." That same year she also testified before the Judiciary Committee that Congress had not only the authority to extend the ERA ratification deadline but also had the "responsibility." She kept that Big ERA Energy up, and in 2018, when asked about the amendment RBG reiterated her support, saying:

"[W]ho are 'We the People'? I would not have been there—half of the population would not have been there. The people who were held in human bondage, Native Americans, were not part of the political constituency. . . . I think the genius of the Constitution is that this concept of 'We the People' has become ever more embracing. And so, I would like to see an Equal Rights Amendment in our Constitution."

RBG remained committed to the ERA to her dying day saying, "I would like my granddaughters, when they pick up the Constitution, to see that notion—that women and men are persons of equal stature—I'd like them to see that is a basic principle of our society."

Another lifelong cause for Justice Ginsburg was giving credit to Pauli Murray's pioneering work. In the very last year of her life, RBG sat down for an interview and had lots of love to give Pauli: "[I] would like to speak about a woman who came to be a role model for me, although we were both adults. Her name was Pauli Murray. . . . [She] wrote an article that was a major influence on me and other women in the '70s. It was called 'Jane Crow and the Law'. . . . [She] spoke about all the artificial barriers that stand in the way of women being able to achieve what their talent and hard work would allow them to achieve. . . . [Pauli] was a woman way ahead of her time."

"WHO ARE 'WE THE PEOPLE'?"

THE NOTORIOUS RBG

Ruth Bader Ginsburg

MARTHA WRIGHT GRIFFITHS

1912–2003

"All I want to be is human and American and have all the same rights and I will shut up."

These discoveries cemented what Martha already suspected—that women weren't just unequal in society, but also they were unequal under law. This knowledge would inform one of her greatest legislative contributions. When US House Judiciary Committee began to deliberate the landmark 1964 Civil

CHAPTER 9
MOTHER OF THE ERA

BORN ON JANUARY 29, 1912, Martha Edna Wright was just eight years old when women gained the constitutional right to vote in 1920. Martha didn't come from wealth, and despite the successes of the suffrage movement, her mom, Lou Ella, knew firsthand that the only way for a woman to not be dependent on her husband was if she was educated. So Lou Ella took on extra jobs to pay for her daughter's college tuition. Her mom's dedication, long hours, and grueling work borne out of a lack of options inspired Martha to spend a lifetime pursuing equal rights for women.

If Lou Ella's goal was to invest in a more equal future—financing Martha's education paid off in spades.

THE ONLY WAY FOR A WOMAN TO NOT BE DEPENDENT ON HER HUSBAND WAS IF SHE WAS EDUCATED.

WITH HER MOTHER'S FINANCIAL help, Martha attended the University of Missouri to pursue a degree in political science. While there, she met and fell hard for Hicks Griffiths, whom she married while still in college at age twenty-one (and would remain married to until death did them part). Following graduation in 1934, the couple moved to Michigan, where they both

A MORE EQUAL FUTURE

A MORE EQUAL

FUTURE

A MORE EQUAL FUTURE

Judge women as individual human beings

attended law school and pursued legal careers. For a few years they operated a law practice in Detroit with a former college classmate, G. Mennen Williams (whose nickname was "Soapy" because his grandfather started a brand of men's toiletries), but after working for the defense department throughout the Second World War, Martha decided to redirect her career—this time, to politics.

Her first attempt at election to the Michigan House of Representatives in 1946 was a bust, but in 1948 she won the first of two terms in the state legislature—becoming one of only two women serving at the time. In 1952, Martha set her sights on a congressional seat but lost the bid. Her former law partner, Soapy, turned out to be a good friend to have. He had been recently elected governor (in large part because of her help with his campaign), and appointed her to be a judge in Detroit. Over the course of her two-year tenure on the bench, Martha oversaw more than four hundred criminal cases. Her experience in the state legislature and as a judge had given her the opportunity to see both sides of the law: making it and implementing it. "It is at least an unusual experience to assist for four years in making the laws of this state, and then sit as a judge of people charged with breaking those laws." But Martha still had her eyes set on Congress, and by 1954, people knew her name and respected her work in the courtroom. Martha's second bid for a federal seat was a success.

As she settled into her new role as a congress-woman, Martha was dumbfounded and angered by some of the

> Martha still had her eyes set on Congress, and by 1954, people knew her name and respected her work in the courtroom.

Amazingly, Martha Wright Griffiths won her congressional seat without the support of the state's Democratic party, which backed a different candidate (whoops!). But they learned their lesson. She would go on to be elected nine more times without facing any serious opposition again.

legal inequities she uncovered. The social security system, for example, would pay benefits to a dead man's dependent children but not to a woman's. Divorced women were ineligible for a pension—no matter how long their former husband had paid into the scheme. Women were obliged to pay tax on their dead husband's estate, but if he was the survivor, he was exempt. Martha had had it, and told her colleagues, "I am tired of paying into a pension fund to support your widow but not my widower." (Even the word for "person whose spouse has died" is gendered! Widow = woman and widower = man.)

These discoveries cemented what Martha already suspected—that women weren't just unequal in society, they were unequal under law. This knowledge would inform one of her greatest legislative contributions. When the US House Judiciary Committee began to deliberate the landmark 1964 Civil Rights Act, she played a big part in developing the gender discrimination amendment to Title VII of the bill. Title VII barred employment discrimination on the basis of race, national origin, color, religion, and—in an eleventh-hour addition thanks to Martha's hard work—also sex. With the help of some now-familiar faces, Alice Paul (page 97) and Pauli

Murray (page 119), Title VII became one of the most seismic legal boons for women in the workplace of the twentieth century. Martha would later push the newly established Equal Employment Opportunity Commission to take it more seriously and vigorously enforce it.

She relied on some deft maneuvering to secure her amendment to the Civil Rights Act. As we know, Democrat Howard Smith of Virginia opposed the bill (because racism) but told Martha and Alice Paul he would work with them to convince Southern congressional members to support a "sex amendment." He was, of course, a double agent who was actually trying to kill the overall bill with what he saw as a misogynist poison pill. Martha knew, however, that if good ol' Howard presented the amendment, he could garner a hundred Southern votes, so she took the gamble. As predicted, when Smith introduced the amendment, the House chamber erupted into male laughter (LOLZ, ladies don't want discrimination). But Martha was ready to rumble.

She took to the floor and said, "I presume that if there had been any necessity to point out that women were a second-class sex, the laughter would have proved it."

In 1961, congresswomen had lobbied Speaker Sam Rayburn to assign a woman to the prominent Ways and Means Committee, which deals with all things related to money. In 1962, Martha became the first woman to be appointed to the committee. She was especially attentive to frequent requests from women on how to overcome discrimination in the workplace.

When an airline stewardess was sacked in 1966 for secretly getting married (which was against the rules), her employers rationalized the firing by telling Martha they wanted stewardesses who were "young, attractive, and single." Never afraid to be direct, Martha sent the CEO a blistering letter asking: "What are you running, an airline, or a whorehouse?"

Martha's sex amendment coup also succeeded with a little help from her friends—one friend in particular, Lyndon B. Johnson, who had unexpectedly attained the presidency in 1963 when President John F. Kennedy was assassinated. She persuaded him to continue to support the Civil Rights Act—even with the word "sex" added in—since it had been such a cornerstone of JFK's legacy and would now be of Johnson's presidency as well. Johnson signed it into law on July 2, 1964, "sex" and all.

(Boom!) She explained that the Civil Rights Act, without the "sex amendment," would protect African American women from race-based discrimination, but not sex discrimination, and that, obviously, no white women would be protected from sex discrimination, either. Driving home her point to Congress (and perhaps one last unfortunate attempt to appeal to racist legislators), she said, "A vote against this amendment today by a white man is a vote against his wife or his widow or his daughter or his sister." Thoroughly chastised, the men voted to pass the measure and the word "sex" was added to the act.

TITLE VII WAS A big victory. But like Alice Paul, Martha Wright Griffiths believed that following the enactment of the Nineteenth Amendment, the Equal Rights Amendment was the next necessary step to guarantee equal justice for all citizens. From 1923 to 1970, the ERA was proposed at every congressional session. Martha herself sponsored the legislation on eight different occasions. For the many times the ERA was proposed, it was stalled for decades through byzantine efforts to bury it and never let it make it out of the Judiciary Committee onto the House floor where legislators could actually bring it to a vote. Like the Nineteenth Amendment, the men tried to kill it by dragging their feet.

But these roadblocks would eventually lead to Martha's finest political plotting. Like Pauli Murray and Ruth Bader Ginsburg (page 136), she'd originally tried to secure women's rights though the courts, but also came to believe that only a constitutional amendment could ensure victory in a system that refused to acknowledge women as "'persons' within the meaning of the Constitution." She thought the ERA would send a message to the Supreme Court, saying specifically to the justices: "Wake up! This is the 20th Century. Before it is over, judge women as individual human beings. They, too, are entitled to the protection of the Constitution, the basic fundamental law of this country."

So in 1970—for the fiftieth anniversary of women winning the constitutional right to vote—Martha pulled out a wild card, an almost forgotten and rarely used congressional mechanism called a "discharge petition," which requires the signatures of a majority of House members and forces legislation out of committee so it can be considered by the whole House of Representatives. She toiled away to win the required 218 members to bring the bill out of committee and onto the floor for general debate and a vote, relentlessly pursuing people at meetings and in the hallways.

With her 218 signatures filed on time, Martha brought the ERA to the House floor on August 10, 1970. "Mr. Speaker," she said, "this is not a battle between the sexes—nor a battle between this body and women. This is a battle with the Supreme Court of the United States." (Martha threw down the guantlet.) With a number of members already out for August recess and not voting, the House passed the ERA by a vote of 352 to 15 (with

Martha Wright Griffiths

"I PRESUME THAT IF THERE HAD BEEN ANY NECESSITY TO POINT OUT THAT WOMEN WERE A SECOND-CLASS SEX, THE LAUGHTER WOULD HAVE PROVED IT."

all the women present—from both parties—voting in favor of the amendment). After some legislative hiccups that killed the ERA's momentum, it fell short in the Senate. Undeterred, Martha then immediately introduced it again the next year in 1971, and it cleared the House for a second time in October. It was approved by the Senate in March 1972. The ERA passed by 354 to 24 in the House and 84 to 8 in the Senate (a margin that is almost unthinkable today).

One major concession Martha felt she had to make in order to get the ERA through Congress that second try was adding a deadline. The ERA was then sent to the states for ratification with a seven-year time limit attached in the proposing clause of the amendment, creating a deadline of 1979 for when it had to have the required number of state ratifications. At the end of the decade when ratification was looking unlikely, Congress extended the ERA time limit by three more years to June 30, 1982 (which RBG personally fought for). Despite all Martha's hard work, the ten-year state ratification process in the 1970s resulted in only thirty-five of the required thirty-eight states needed for ratification, but her work on the ERA still remained

When Martha cornered the Democratic Whip, Thomas Hale Boggs Sr. of Louisiana, to get his signature, "he promised to sign as Number 200, convinced that I would never make it." But she continued to play the hand she was dealt. He soon found out that betting against her was never a good idea, and "when [she] had Number 199 signed up, [she] rushed to his office, and Hale Boggs became number 200." Martha cashed in all her chips!

EQUAL RIGHTS AMEND- MENT

BY THE NUMBERS

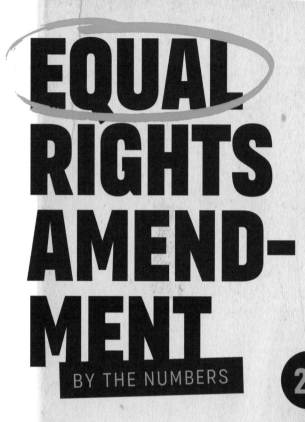

 24 WORDS IN ITS MAIN CLAUSE

 38 NUMBER OF STATES
NEEDED TO RATIFY

28 TWENTY-EIGHTH AMENDMENT
TO THE CONSTITUTION

 1923 WHEN IT WAS FIRST INTRODUCED

 1972 WHEN IT FINALLY PASSED
IN CONGRESS

her crowning moment and cemented her legacy as one of the most effective women's rights activists of the twentieth century.

In 1974, with the ERA successfully through Congress and making its way through the states at a rapid pace, Martha declined to run for an eleventh congressional term and instead continued to fight for the ERA at the state level. Opponents of ratification trotted out a whole parade of horribles against the ERA, like unisex bathrooms, economic ruin for house-wives, mandatory same-sex marriages, forced combat duty for women, and unfettered abortions. (None of which were true.) Martha Wright Griffiths and Phyllis Schlafly, a conservative woman who was the founder of the STOP ERA campaign, sharply debated the issue at a national forum in 1976. Schlafly was a shrewd opponent of the ERA. (More on her on page 185.)

Deadlines for amendments are not required by the Constitution. Deadlines started being added with the prohibition amendment because the legislators felt immense pressure from the anti-alcohol movement to pass it, but were all boozehounds and didn't want it to actually get ratified. (Plot twist: It did anyway.) The most recent amendment to the Constitution, the Twenty-Seventh Amendment, never had a deadline, and although it was first proposed by James Madison in 1789, it was not ratified until 1992—202 years, 7 months, and 10 days later. Many ERA proponents think that since the Constitution doesn't require it, and 200 years is not too long to wait for an amendment—a deadline on the ERA shouldn't keep women out of the Constitution, either.

AFTER LEAVING CONGRESS, Martha kept up her breakneck pace. In 1982, she became the first woman elected lieutenant governor of Michigan when she was invited to run with James Johnston Blanchard. They were reelected in 1986,

"I WOULD LIKE TO KNOW THEY HAVE GIVEN WOMEN THE SAME BENEFITS AND PROMOTIONS AS MEN."

but the third time 'round Blanchard secretly decided to drop Martha (who was now seventy-eight years old) from the ticket. (Never trust a man with his eyes on power!) Governor Blanchard said he'd dropped her because of her age and ill health, but she countered that it was women and the elderly who had put him into office in the first place. Martha shot back: "He has a right to do what he wants to do. And after the election, we'll see what he should have done." He lost the election. "I don't know if I feel vindicated, but I think it clearly shows that I won it for him the first two times," Martha tartly said after Governor Blanchard's defeat.

Not yet ready to retire after her terms as lieutenant governor, Martha resumed practicing law. She made it clear what it would take to keep her quiet: "Before I leave this Earth, I would like to know they have given women the same benefits and promotions as men. All I want to be is human and American and have all the same rights and I will shut up." She died in 2003 at her home in Armada, Michigan, at the age of ninety-one, after having done everything in her power to achieve equality. She'd grown up as the Equal Rights Amendment itself had developed—both coming into the public political discourse and making waves. She had spent nearly a century fighting for equal rights for women. She remained child-free during her sixty-two-year marriage, but Martha Wright Griffiths protected and nurtured something equally impactful, gaining her the title "Mother of the ERA."

NEVER TRUST A MAN WITH HIS EYES ON POWER!

Martha Wright Griffiths

MARTHA'S SEX AMENDMENT COUP... SUCCEEDED

WITH A LITTLE HELP FROM HER FRIENDS.

ELIZABETH HOLTZMAN

The OG AOC

One of the main people who kept the ERA languishing in committee for decades in Congress was Representative Emanuel Celler from Brooklyn. Even though he was a Democrat, he was one of the most anti-equality members of Congress. As the powerful chairman of the US House Judiciary Committee, he had refused to hold a hearing on the ERA for over thirty years. Facing a huge amount of pressure from the women's movement, he finally passed it through his committee but still tried everything he could to defeat it.

Pulling an AOC move long before Alexandria Ocasio-Cortez was born, a young, unknown pro-ERA candidate named Elizabeth Holtzman challenged Celler in his 1972 primary, right after the ERA had passed in Congress. At that point, Celler was an octogenarian, and exceedingly cranky. He said Elizabeth was "as irritating as a hangnail." But that hangnail candidate won by just 635 votes. (Never doubt that your vote matters!) By opposing the ERA, and being totally oblivious to both his constituents and the power of young women, Celler became the most senior representative in US history to lose a primary, and at thirty-one years old, Elizabeth Holtzman became the youngest woman ever elected to Congress. (AOC later broke that record at age twenty-nine.)

Celler had serious delusions of grandeur and compared Holtzman's victory to "a toothpick toppling the Washington Monument." (Boy, bye.) *Time* magazine had a decidedly different take on events and dubbed her "Liz the Lion Killer." Immediately after taking office, she replaced him on the powerful Judiciary Committee. In 1978, Elizabeth led the fight to secure a three-year extension of the 1979 ERA ratification deadline. (He wasn't dead yet, but Celler was preemptively rolling over in his grave.) Elizabeth Holtzman is still alive today—and still fighting for the ERA.

Elizabeth Holtzman

PATSY TAKEMOTO MINK

"It is easy enough to vote right and be consistently with the majority. But it is more often more important to be ahead of the majority and this means being willing to cut the first furrow in the ground and stand alone for a while if necessary."

1927–2002

Never one to sit idle, Patsy joined forces with two other congresswomen and they wasted no time in m their presence felt among their male coll Harkening back to her college days, Patsy org protest against banning women from congressional gym. Patsy's male coll particularly fond of using the pool—in th too much for the democratic process to your pants on?" Patsy asked. Appa members of

CHAPTER 10
FIRST, BUT NOT LAST

PATSY TAKEMOTO MINK'S PARENTS, Suematso and Mitama Takemoto, were second-generation Japanese immigrants. In 1941, Patsy was just fourteen when the Japanese attacked Pearl Harbor in her home state of Hawai'i and the United States entered World War II. Life in the Pacific amid the strong anti-Asian sentiment that swept through the United States and its territories following the attack was the backdrop for many of Patsy's formative experiences. In the aftermath of Pearl Harbor, her father, a civil engineer, was taken away in the night and questioned by authorities. Although he returned home the next day, he would later burn all his Japanese mementos in order to protect himself from false claims of anti-Americanism. "It made me realize that one actually could not take citizenship and the promise of the U.S. Constitution for granted," Patsy said. Ultimately 120,000 Japanese Americans would be imprisoned in internment camps.

In 1944, the exclusion order leading to the internment of Japanese Americans was upheld as constitutional by the Supreme Court in the case *Korematsu v. United States*. Only three justices dissented, arguing that the exclusion order legitimized racism and violated the Equal Protection Clause of the

"ONE ACTUALLY COULD NOT TAKE THE PROMISE OF THE U.S. CONSTITUTION FOR GRANTED."

Fourteenth Amendment. Patsy learned while still a teenager that the Constitution was certainly not infallible, and she would dedicate her life to making our legal system protect more people.

——————

PATSY WAS BORN IN Maui on December 6, 1927, and grew up idolizing the family physician, and just like Matilda Joslyn Gage (page 39), dreamed of becoming a doctor. From a young age, she always wanted to help others heal. At school, she was an active student. As a high school senior, she became the first female elected student body president and graduated valedictorian of her class in 1944. Even with her activism on campus, she remained focused on her goal of obtaining a medical degree.

But Patsy's path was far from easy once she got to college. After graduating from high school, she enrolled in the University of Nebraska. There, Patsy faced racial discrimination when she was placed in student housing segregated by race. She helped form the group Unaffiliated Students of the University of Nebraska for students of color who were barred from joining sororities and fraternities. Eventually the group succeeded in persuading the university to change its racist policies. Later, Patsy transferred to the University of Hawai'i to complete her undergraduate degree, where she remained active in student politics and participated in the student constitutional convention. She was also keeping on top of her heavy premed course load, in addition to a second full-time load—dismantling systems of oppression wherever she went!

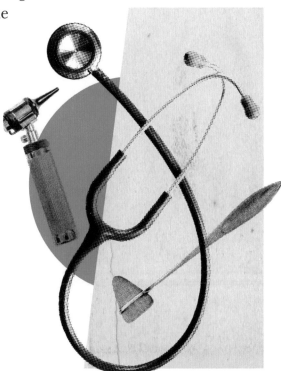

Although Patsy had begun to question what her professional path might be, she was determined to see through her dream of becoming a doctor. She filled out applications to more than a dozen medical schools but despite an incredible academic performance, she was rejected by every single one. In many of the letters she received, it was explicitly indicated she was denied entrance because she was a woman. "It was the most devastating disappointment of my life," Patsy later recalled. "That I could have spent my whole educational experience . . . geared toward one thing and then have all the schools . . . say 'no, can't have you.'" The blatantly discriminatory slew of rejections provided a spark for social change that turned into a bonfire of rage and determination. Now Patsy wanted to make justice less of a hobby and more of a career; she turned her aspirations from medicine to law and dedicated herself to fixing societal ailments.

When Patsy arrived at the University of Chicago Law School in the fall of 1951, she was one of only two women in her class. She had, she believed, been admitted in part due to a "foreign quota"—despite having been born in Hawai'i and therefore being a US citizen (once again, off to a very racist start). While there, she met and married a graduate student, John Mink, and gave birth to their daughter, Gwendolyn, in 1952. After Patsy graduated from law school in 1951, she applied to work at law firms in Chicago but not a single one was willing to hire a woman—much less the mother of a young child, not to mention an Asian American woman in an interracial marriage. Just by being herself, the deck was stacked very high against her. Patsy faced similar obstacles when she applied to jobs at law firms in the Northeast and the mid-Atlantic—there was no misogyny-free zone in the United States. Finally, she and John decided to move their family back to Hawai'i, where Patsy thought she would have better luck securing work with the law degree she had fought so incredibly hard to earn.

But in Hawai'i, Patsy discovered she wasn't even allowed to sit for the bar exam. To sit for the exam, the examinee needed to be a resident of Hawai'i, and despite having been born and raised there, when Patsy married her Pennsylvania-born husband, she'd apparently automatically forfeited her Hawai'ian residency (taking on his instead). At just twenty-six years old, Patsy put her new law degree to work and challenged the residency requirement. She won her first legal victory defending herself from discrimination!

Despite her victory and admission to the bar, Patsy still struggled to find employment. Eventually she decided to set up her own practice; she would be the boss she had been searching for all over the country. For her very first legal case, she accepted a fish as payment. Being self-employed also allowed Patsy the time to engage in her other interests—ripping white supremacy and patriarchy to shreds. She joined in Hawai'ian territorial politics, working for local candidates at the state level and founding the Oahu Young Democrats.

Did you know that Hawai'i once had a legit queen? Her name was Queen Lili'uokalani. In 1893, her monarchy was overthrown by pro-American landowners who wanted to see the islands annexed by the United States. Queen Lili'uokalani attempted to secure a new constitution that would have reinstated the monarchy's authority and restored voting rights to native Hawai'ians, but, alas, it didn't work. Not one to go down without a fight, while she was in prison for her acts to resist colonization, Lili'uokalani wrote a book called *Hawai'i's Story by Hawai'i's Queen*. In 1898, after five years as an independent republic, the United States "annexed" Hawai'i, just as those who overthrew the queen had wanted, making it a US territory. Defiant to the end, Queen Lili'uokalani boycotted the ceremony. Still a territory all those years later, Patsy Takemoto Mink first served in the territorial legislature.

HAWAI'I WASN'T EVEN A state yet (it became one in 1959) when Patsy decided to run for Congress. She had worked as an attorney for the territorial legislature; then she was elected to the chamber in 1956 and 1958 and served in the Hawai'ian territorial senate from 1958 to 1959, so she was well qualified. When Patsy was sworn in to the Hawai'ian legislature, she was the only female lawmaker, and was the first Japanese American to serve in the body. However, in spite of her success, an influential Hawai'ian politician by the name of John Anthony Burns, who had once been Patsy's mentor, decided to work behind the scenes and pit his favored candidate against her. (Again, never trust a man with his eyes on power!) Even though Burns was formidable, she didn't bow down to his or the party's pressure, but yet again, Patsy found herself shut out of a boys' club. She lost the race.

In 1964, Hawai'i got a second congressional seat and Patsy mounted a grassroots campaign. As a candidate for the territorial legislature, she had gone door-to-door asking people for their votes (a novel approach at the time), and she decided she would do the same as she sought to represent Hawai'i in Washington, DC. This time, her people-powered campaign and personal approach worked—she won!

When the Minks arrived in Washington in 1965, it made for an enormous shift in their lifestyle. Beyond the cultural and climate differences between Hawai'i and Washington, DC (the capital isn't exactly known for its #islandvibes), the Minks also faced other difficulties. The family first settled in nearby Arlington, Virginia, but interracial marriages like theirs were still illegal. It would be another two years before the Supreme Court made its decision striking down the state's anti-miscegenation law in *Loving v. Virginia*—and though she had come to Washington to make a difference, it gave her a view of just how much still desperately needed to change.

Representative Patsy Takemoto Mink was 1 of only 12 women (out of 535 seats) in Congress when she took office on January 4, 1965. Patsy's swearing-in at the US Capitol was historic; not only was she the first Asian American woman to serve in Congress, but she was the first woman of color ever. In addition to being from the youngest state, at age thirty-seven, she was the entire body's youngest member. Even though she was under intense scrutiny during her early years in Congress, Patsy didn't deviate from the issues that had captured her attention as a lawmaker in Hawai'i, including better childcare and early-childhood education, offering education that's more equitable for girls of all ages, and women's equality. In fact, she introduced the first federal childcare legislation and cosponsored bills that established student loans, bilingual education, special education reforms, and the Head Start program.

Never one to sit idle, Patsy joined forces with two other congress-women and they wasted no time in making their presence felt among their male colleagues. Harkening back to her college days, Patsy organized a protest against banning women from using the congressional gym. Patsy's male colleagues were particularly fond of using the pool—in the nude. "Is it too much for the democratic process to ask you to put your pants on?" Patsy asked. Apparently, for some members of Congress, it was.

———

AS A CHILD GROWING up in the Pacific in the 1940s, Patsy's political consciousness was shaped by war, and as a politician in the Hawai'ian legislature, she was a vocal opponent of nuclear testing in the region. As an up-and-coming congresswoman, Patsy was an early and vocal opponent of the Vietnam War and, even at home with her family, she emphasized the importance of nonviolence in political action. Almost a decade later, Patsy's connection to the anti-war movement would see her become the first Asian American woman to run for president when she was recruited by Oregon Democrats as an anti-war candidate. Her daughter, Gwendolyn, who became a feminist scholar of American politics, said, "My mother taught me that an election is not an end in itself, but rather an opening to do the hard work of securing justice, peace and the well-being of all." Patsy went into public service to make things better for everyone, not just herself.

SHE EMPHASIZED THE IMPORTANCE OF NONVIOLENCE IN POLITICAL ACTION.

Even as Patsy enjoyed a successful career as an elected official and the opportunities it brought her to help the people of Hawai'i and women across the country, her early experiences with prejudice were never far from her mind. In 1969, Patsy was involved in a series of legislative reforms that helped advance women's rights. These efforts culminated in her introduction of what we now know as Title IX (page 168).

The summer before Patsy arrived in the House, Congress passed the landmark 1964 Civil Rights Act. The act remains a pivotal piece of labor legislation that outlaws discrimination on the basis of race, color, religion, national origin, or sex in employment, schools, or places of "public accommodation," such as recreation facilities or retail stores. Since its original passage, the Civil Rights Act has also been amended to include protections against discrimination based on sexual orientation and gender identity.

Equality for women across the federal level remained imperative for Patsy and many of her colleagues in the House and in the Senate. As they had refused to protect Japanese Americans during WWII, the courts still refused to even consider that the Fourteenth Amendment's Equal Protections Clause might also extend to protect women. This underscored the need for the Equal Rights Amendment to formally enshrine women's equality into the Constitution.

When Martha Griffiths's hard work finally got the ERA out of committee and to the floor for a vote, Patsy championed it. She believed the ERA would help get "extensive legislation" passed at the federal and state levels to "eliminate situations which are discriminatory in effect." When people argued that the ERA was redundant, she countered, "[There] are worse things than

In 1970, Patsy became the first person to oppose a Supreme Court nominee on the basis of discrimination against women. In her testimony before the Senate regarding Nixon–nominated George Harrold Carswell, Patsy said, "I am here to testify against his confirmation on the grounds that his appointment constitutes an affront to the women of America." Carswell had refused to hear a discrimination case about a woman who had been denied a job because she was a woman with children, and Patsy explained that "Judge Carswell demonstrated a total lack of understanding of the concept of equality." Her daughter, Gwendolyn, later recalled, "It felt very momentous and risky. Nobody had ever talked about sexism or misogyny for objecting to a Supreme Court justice." Carswell got the boot from the Senate and never became a justice. Harry Blackmun, who later wrote the majority opinion in *Roe v. Wade*, which granted women legal access to abortion in the United States, got the seat instead. Thanks, Patsy!

redundancy, among them the lack of action by our executive, legislative and judicial bodies to put into effect the equal rights safeguards already in the Constitution."

Patsy saw the ERA as a firm foundation, and just the first step for equality. She said it would provide "constitutional backing" for bold, transformative laws needed to protect and support women and girls. When the ERA was finally passed by Congress on March 22, 1972, it was midafternoon. Because of the huge time difference between Hawai'i and DC, the Hawai'i Senate and House voted their approval shortly after noon their time the very same day. In part due to her influence and support, Patsy's state was the first to ratify the ERA.

In 1975, Patsy sponsored a congressional act to give $5 million of public funds for a National Women's Conference. A kind of feminist political Woodstock, it was held in Houston in 1977 and was a major turning point for the feminist movement. Many positive things happened at the conference. Delegates voted to support lesbian rights, which had been a major divisive issue up to that point, but anti-ERA Phyllis Schlafly (page 185) also seized the opportunity to grab the spotlight with a counter-conference in a nearby stadium to give the perception that equal amounts of American women opposed the ERA as supported it—this was and still is a vicious lie!

When it came time for Patsy to run for her seventh term in 1977, instead of coasting to what would have been an assured victory, she stepped up to a new challenge and decided to run for the US Senate. This ultimately unsuccessful bid set off a time in her life that took her away from the halls of Congress, but never far away from politics or her commitment to helping fight against inequality. In 1977, President Jimmy Carter appointed Patsy to the post of Assistant Secretary of State for Oceans and International Environmental and Scientific Affairs. Then she served as president of a Democratic action group in DC, and then she returned to Hawai'i to serve on the Honolulu City Council. Not one for rest, Patsy also took a stab at running for both governor and mayor of Honolulu but didn't win either race.

Finally, Patsy returned to the US House in 1990. The following year, she yet again mounted a campaign to oppose a nominee based on discrimination against women. She voiced opposition to Clarence Thomas's nomination to the Supreme Court after Anita Hill, a former aide to Thomas, accused him of sexual harassment. Alongside six of her fellow feminist lawmakers, Patsy led a protest march to the Senate to demand they delay Thomas's confirmation hearing until all charges could be investigated. After their protest, Ms. Hill was permitted to testify, but despite her courage in speaking up, the accused sexual harasser was narrowly confirmed and sits on the bench to this day.

Patsy would go on to serve in Congress for another eleven years, until her death on September 28, 2002. That year, following her death, the House went on to rename Title IX the "Patsy T. Mink

John Mink

Patsy Takemoto Mink

PATSY'S PURSUIT OF A NEW PATH AND A NEW DREAM IN THE FACE OF ADVERSITY ALLOWED FUTURE GENERATIONS OF WOMEN TO ACHIEVE THEIR OWN.

Equal Opportunity in Education Act." In 2014, she was posthumously awarded the Presidential Medal of Freedom by President Barack Obama.

PATSY TAKEMOTO MINK may never have realized her ambition to become a doctor, but her work and her advocacy succeeded in helping invent the remedy for some of the many inequalities that women faced, and continue to grapple with, in the United States. In total, she had served twenty-four years (twelve terms) in Congress. Despite the many struggles and setbacks throughout her life, Patsy's pursuit of a new path and a new dream in the face of adversity allowed future generations of women to achieve their own—she was the first woman of color in Congress, but happy not to be the last.

TITLE IX
Equal Education

The Women's Education Equity Act, or what we now call Title IX, arose out of the necessity of those fighting for women's rights in the late 1960s and early 1970s to, essentially, divide and conquer the sexism deeply entrenched in America's federal legislation. Separate bills were devised to address the range of inequalities that left women—and men—without the protection of the law, from social security earnings to what classes they could or could not take in school, like auto shop and home economics.

With Patsy at the helm, she and her colleagues worked for months to reconcile hundreds of differences between the House and Senate versions of the bills. The legislation was part of an omnibus bill (a single bill containing several pieces of legislation) called the Higher Education Act, which also included provisions for measures including ethnic studies programs and school busing initiatives. The bill read: "No person in the United States shall, on the basis of sex, be excluded from participation in, be denied the benefits of, or be subjected to discrimination under any education program or activity receiving federal financial assistance."

With just thirty-seven words, Patsy had changed the future of American higher education, by prohibiting sex discrimination in educational institutions that receive federal funding (the vast majority of schools).

This helps protect girls from sexual assault and harassment on campus, as well as mandates equal funding and investment into female athletic programs. While Title IX is well-known for its positive impact on women in sports, it also opened the doors for women to attend medical school—such a special victory for Patsy to have won. Title IX serves as a reminder to generations of students, teachers, parents, administrators, coaches, lawyers, and doctors that their access to equal rights and education has not always been a guarantee. Moreover, it remains one of many reminders of the work that still needs to be done to ensure these same rights are guaranteed to all in the Constitution.

Patsy Takemoto Mink

WITH JUST THIRTY-SEVEN WORDS, PATSY HAD CHANGED THE FUTURE OF... HIGHER EDUCATION

BARBARA

JORDAN

"What the people want is very <u>simple</u>—they want an America as good as its (promise.)"

1936–1996

arbara Jordan started experiencin
rejudice even as she came out of he
other's womb into Texas at the heigh
f the Great Depression in 1936. As soon
s the successful delivery was complete,
er own father asked, "Why is she so
ark?" From that moment, skin and
ody—color, hue, texture, size,
ondition—began to determine how
eople would react to Barbara. But,

CHAPTER 11

WE THE PEOPLE

FOR A POLITICIAN, PUBLIC FIGURE, and folk hero, Barbara Jordan was an uncommonly private person. She inspired millions with her commanding voice and incredible talent for oration, but most never knew anything about her personal struggles. She started suffering from multiple sclerosis in 1973 but didn't publicly disclose the diagnosis. She went on as if nothing was wrong.

She was a lesbian and shared her life with Nancy Earl, her partner of over twenty years, but because of advice from advisors who said it would damage her political aspirations, she never publicly came out during her lifetime. Barbara was, however, straightforward about her sexual orientation in private to those close to her. A friend said, "She never denied who she was. It just was not the public's need to know."

Barbara and Nancy, who met on a camping trip, had a beautiful love story. In her autobiography, her words about seeing Nancy for the first time leap off the page: "At some point Nancy Earl arrived, and that was the first time that we would meet face to face. . . . Nancy and I sat there playing the guitar; we had just met but we were singing and drinking and having a swell time . . . I had had a great time and enjoyed myself very much.

SHE INSPIRED MILLIONS WITH HER COMMANDING VOICE AND INCREDIBLE TALENT FOR ORATION.

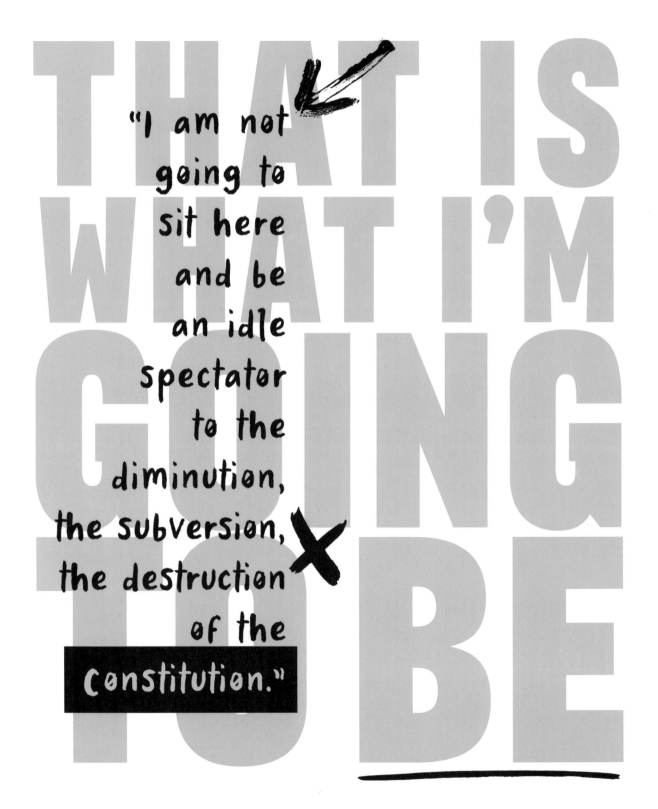

I remember I thought: this is something I would like to repeat." (Swoon!) After that camping trip, in what is known as U-Hauling in lesbian parlance, the two soon built a house together in Austin, Texas.

Because of her MS, Barbara had to do physical therapy. She nearly drowned once while doing physical therapy in their backyard swimming pool, but Nancy found her floating before it was too late and literally dove into the pool to save her life. The disease also forced Barbara to retire from Congress. Nancy left Texas to work in Barbara's office with her in Washington, DC, during her last year there. Records show that Nancy had the title "special assistant" and was the second-highest-paid person in Barbara's office. (Scandalous!) Always by her side, she wrote Barbara's speeches and dealt with the press.

Barbara was lauded for fighting for the most marginalized, and the public had no idea how marginalized Barbara herself was. Unable to be clear about her sexual orientation and her romantic relationship during her lifetime, the silence was broken in Barbara's obituary in the *Houston Chronicle*, which listed Nancy Earl, whom it called her "longtime companion," among her survivors—putting the truth on the record for the first time.

Barbara was lauded for fighting for the most margrinalized, and the public had no idea how marginalized Barbara herself was.

BARBARA JORDAN STARTED EXPERIENCING prejudice even as she came out of her mother's womb and into Texas at the height of the Great Depression in 1936. As soon as the successful delivery was complete, her own father asked, "Why is she so dark?" From that moment, skin and body—color, hue, texture, size, condition—began to determine how people would react

Colorism is a form of discrimination that exists within a racial or ethnic group. Colorism privileges people with lighter skin, places disadvantages on people with darker skin tones, and is harmful to all.

to Barbara. But from the very start, she refused to let their prejudice get in her way.

In the early 1950s, as she attended the all-Black Phillis Wheatley High School (love to see that Phillis legacy going strong!), Barbara's physical features limited her choices. She felt her teachers favored lighter-skinned students, who were given the majority of honors, awards, and opportunities. They also escaped the harshness of encounters with law enforcement. A common saying in her segregated neighborhood was "The lighter the skin, the lighter the sentence."

As a teenager, Barbara did normal things: attending slumber parties, going out to sing the 1950s version of karaoke, and getting her driver's license so she could drive her friends around. But by the time she was a teenager, Barbara had also been confronted by all of America's negative messages about skin color. And there was one consistent message: "The world had decided that we were all Negro, but that some of us were more Negro than others."

Barbara remembered, "The whole system . . . was saying to us that you achieved more, you went further, you had a better chance, you got the awards, if you were not black-black with kinky hair." She went on, "Black was bad and you didn't want to be black, and so the message we were getting was that you were really in tough shape and it was too bad that you were so unfortunate that your skin was totally black and there was no light there anywhere." But Barbara never let outside expectations amper her ambition—she was smart and she knew it. She had boundless belief in herself.

Barbara first found her voice on the high school debate team. When the noted African American lawyer Edith Spurlock Sampson of Chicago spoke at a career day program at her school. Barbara set a goal that day saying, "That's it. That is what I'm going to be." She graduated from Phillis Wheatley High in 1952 and was a member of the inaugural class at Texas Southern University (TSU), a Black college in her hometown of Houston that was hastily created by the Texas legislature to avoid having to integrate the University of Texas. At TSU, Barbara became a champion debater and helped the team to national renown. When Harvard's debate team came to town, TSU famously beat them.

Graduating from TSU in 1956, Barbara was accepted to Boston University's law school. One of only two Black women in her class, Barbara proudly earned her law degree three years later. She passed the Massachusetts and Texas bars and returned to Houston to open a law office on her mother and father's kitchen table.

WHILE WORKING AT HER law practice, Barbara started to make a go in the political scene in Texas, despite the three strikes against her—being a woman, being Black, and having

A Baptist preacher with traditional ideas about a woman's place, Barbara's father scolded the teacher who encouraged her to become a lawyer. When the teacher asked what her plan was, Barbara defiantly replied, "I am big and fat and black and ugly, and I'll never have a man problem."

But she knew she could not afford college on her own, so she resolved to "do exactly what [my father] tells me to until I am twenty-one years old and then I'll do what I damn well please." And that she did.

heavily melanated skin. In 1962, she ran unsuccessfully for the Texas House of Representatives. In 1964 (the same year the Civil Rights Act passed in Congress), Barbara ran for the Texas House again. Again, she lost. Hoping that the third time would be the charm—and after a court ordered redistricting that created a new district of largely people of color voters—she ran in 1966 for the Texas State Senate. This time she won, beating out a white man! She became the first Black woman to ever serve in the Texas State Senate and the first Black person of any gender to serve since 1883.

Barbara's colleagues in the Texas Senate thought so highly of her they commissioned her portrait by Black artist Edsel Cramer to hang in the state capitol alongside portraits of Davy Crockett, Sam Houston, Lyndon B. Johnson, and other distinguised statesmen. When a fellow senator told Barbara, "Senator, the only thing missing in [your] portrait is your voice; without your voice, it just isn't you," she used her characteristic humor and quick wit, responding: "Senator, these walls have been needing a touch of color, and when my painting hangs amid the august people on the walls of this chamber, believe me, it's gonna talk."

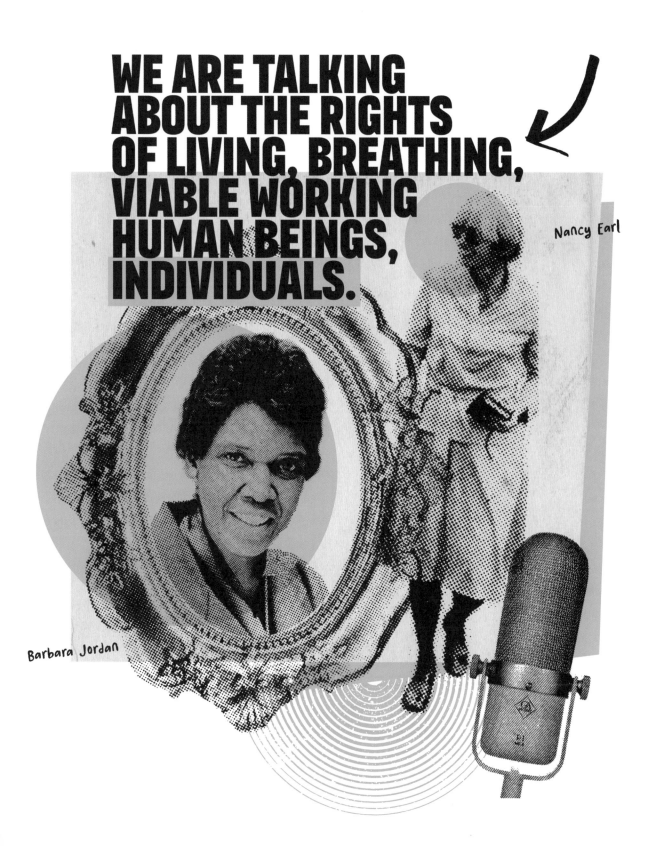

WE ARE TALKING ABOUT THE RIGHTS OF LIVING, BREATHING, VIABLE WORKING HUMAN BEINGS, INDIVIDUALS.

Nancy Earl

Barbara Jordan

"When the document was completed on the seventeenth of September 1787 I was not included in that 'We the People.'"

In 1967, Barbara met fellow Texan and president Lyndon B. Johnson at a meeting for civil rights leaders in Washington. As the country was battling racist gerrymandering in all the states, President Johnson directed a new congressional district be created in Houston, and when Barbara entered the race, LBJ campaigned for her in person. In November 1972—the same year the ERA passed in Congress—Barbara was elected to the US House.

She was the first Black woman from the South ever elected to Congress (the first Black woman, ever, was Shirley Chisholm from New York), and the first Black woman ever to serve on the powerful Judiciary Committee. While still a freshman in the House, Barbara rose to national prominence during the Watergate hearings as Richard Nixon's presidency was starting to crumble. Americans were riveted to their television sets across the country as Barbara stood to present the opening remarks to the House Judiciary Committee. After thanking the chairman for allowing junior members to speak, she began:

> Earlier today, we heard the beginning of the Preamble to the Constitution of the United States, "We the people." It is a very eloquent beginning. But when the document was completed on the seventeenth of September 1787 I was not included in that "We the People." . . . But throughout the process of amendment, interpretation and court decision I have finally been included in "We, the People."

> Today, I am an inquisitor; I believe hyperbole would not be fictional and not overstate the solemnness that I feel right now. My faith in the Constitution is whole, it is complete, it is total. I am not going to sit here and be an idle spectator to the diminution, the subversion, the destruction of the Constitution.

If the impeachment provision in the Constitution of the United States will not reach the offenses charged here, then perhaps that eighteenth century Constitution should be abandoned to a twentieth century paper shredder.

Barbara's impeachment address helped lead to the resignation of Nixon on August 8, 1974. He was the first US president ever to step down, and while Nixon got the boot, Barbara got a boost. She got truckloads of fan mail at her congressional office. One enthusiastic supporter took out twenty-five billboards all across Houston that said, "Thank you, Barbara Jordan, for explaining the Constitution to us." She became so popular that she would draw the kind of clamoring crowds that rock stars get, with people following her and tearing at her clothes.

During her political tenure, she used her knowledge of the Constitution to help bring about equality. She worked on legislation promoting women's rights, including sponsoring bills that championed the poor and people of color. As a congresswoman, she sponsored legislation to broaden the Voting Rights Act of 1965 to cover Mexican Americans in Texas and expand its protections. She cosponsored a bill that would

Edsel Cramer spent years studying the faces of his subjects, isolating the elements of their faces and putting them back together on canvas, and he did the same with Barbara Jordan. Cramer remembered, "There are fine lines etched around her eyes, the sort of lines that mean stress, hard work, and determination. . . . She is simply so big—both in size and personality. I just couldn't paint normal scale no matter how hard I tried. . . . I couldn't help but make her larger than life."

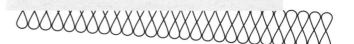

Eleanor Smeal served as the president of NOW from 1977–1982, pivotal years for the ERA. As president, one of her first orders of business was to spearhead the successful effort to add a lesbian rights plank to the national platform at the Houston Women's Conference (which Patsy Mink helped fund).

She played a key role in convincing Representative Elizabeth Holtzman (page 152) to propose that Congress extend the deadline on ratification. Exhibiting both brains and political brawn, Eleanor led the 1978 March for the ERA, which brought over one hundred thousand marchers to Washington and helped push Congress to extend the deadline to 1982. She went on to found the Feminist Majority Foundation in 1987 and is the only ERA advocate alive who worked directly with Alice Paul (page 97) on the amendment and continues to fight for the ERA to this day.

have granted housewives Social Security benefits because they performed the critical work of keeping households running and childcare—a major cause of the second wave feminist movement.

And so it is no surprise that in 1978, with the ERA's initial seven-year deadline for ratification by three-quarters of the states fast approaching, Barbara was one of the main congressional leaders advocating for a three-year extension in order to allow more time for the remaining required states to ratify the amendment. She revered the Constitution, but always fought to make it better and more inclusive, arguing, "The Equal Rights Amendment poses no danger to our liberties; exactly the opposite. The Equal Rights Amendment proposes to fulfill our liberties."

Men in power had kept women out of the Constitution for so long—since Abigail Adams had been shouting at them to "Remember the ladies!"—that ERA proponents needed to extend the initial deadline Congress had attached to it, in order to fight back against two centuries of entrenched opposition to equality. In 1978, as nearly one hundred thousand people marched on Washington in support of the ERA, Barbara argued forcefully before the House Judiciary Committee for the deadline extension to pass, saying:

The Equal Rights Amendment is a mandate for change. . . . It has as much potential for affecting our political, economic, social and psychological lives as we may want to ascribe to it in the future. It is kinetic. The Equal Rights Amendment is for men and women. It is a constructive force for liberating the minds of men and the place of women.

The Equal Rights Amendment is about human values. It defines the standard by which future Congresses, legislatures, Presidents, Governors and courts will define human relationships. It amends the equal protection values of the Fourteenth Amendment beyond race, color and national origin to include gender. It is about equality, and freedom and the pursuit of happiness.

I favor the Equal Rights Amendment and I favor extending the time limit for its ratification.

The men of Congress treated the entire endeavor like child's play, saying, "the game is almost over and the proponents of the ERA are not winning." But Barbara countered, "It is no 'game.' We are talking about the rights of living, breathing, viable working human beings, individuals. We are talking about the Constitution of the United States, something which needs to be done to make it still more perfect. It is no game."

The deadline extension passed.

"THE EQUAL RIGHTS AMENDMENT IS ABOUT HUMAN VALUES."

BARBARA JORDAN LIVED AS A PIONEER AND PROPHET.

FROM THE HIGH SCHOOL debate team to the halls of Congress, Barbara Jordan mastered her craft of oration and inspiration. Her voice was much of her image. It underscored her dignity, and it honestly scared the hell out of people. On hearing it for the first time, one awed young woman said, "I turned on my television set and thought I was listening to God." Congressman Andrew Young of Georgia said her voice sounded "like the heavens have opened up."

In each of her speeches, she articulated themes dear to the hearts of Democrats with a clear focus on the fundamental values of liberty. She was the first Black woman to give the keynote address at the Democratic National Convention when Jimmy Carter was nominated in 1976. (She was so good that even though she wasn't a candidate, she got one delegate's vote for president!) She gave an address again at the convention that nominated Bill Clinton in 1992, where she spoke of the centrality of community and responsibility to the American Dream. She fused that theme with a message of concern for the poor and most marginalized, who were always top of mind to her.

Ultimately her battle with MS forced her to retire from Congress in 1979. She went

"THE EQUAL RIGHTS AMENDMENT PROPOSES TO FULFILL OUR LIBERTIES."

on to become a professor at the University of Texas (now integrated!) and an active public speaker and advocate, amassing twenty-five honorary degrees—including ones from Harvard and Princeton. She died on January 17, 1996, and the headline of her obituary in the *Houston Chronicle* read: A VOICE FOR JUSTICE DIES; BARBARA JORDAN LIVED AS A PIONEER AND PROPHET.

President Clinton, who later awarded her the Medal of Freedom, the highest honor for a civilian, spoke at her funeral about a time he had given a speech at the University of Texas. "I walked out into that vast arena and there were seventeen thousand people there, but I could only see one—Barbara Jordan smiling at me. And there I was about to give a speech to her about race and the Constitution. It was the nearest experience on this earth to the pastor giving a sermon with God in the audience." Barbara's beloved Nancy was sitting with her family at the service to hear the president of the United States sing her praises. Breaking barriers—even in death—she became the first African American to be buried among the governors, senators, and congressmembers in the Texas State Cemetery. In the decades after Barbara's incredible advocacy, the ERA went into hibernation. The 1982 deadline came and went. Feminist leaders focused on getting more women in Congress. But a small group of dedicated ERA activists never gave up on achieving constitutional equality.

PHYLLIS SCHLAFLY

Foot Soldier of the Patriarchy

The men determined to stop the ERA had been working against it on the state and federal level for decades. In the late 1970s, when it seemed on the precipice of success, they needed a new approach—one that changed the narrative as *Men v. Women* (a battle they were losing) to *Women v. Women*. They needed a female foot soldier. Enter Phyllis Schlafly.

Phyllis had earned degrees from Washington University in Saint Louis and from Radcliffe, the sister school of the then all-male Harvard. During World War II, when she was in her early twenties, she worked as a ballistics gunner and technician at the largest ammunition plant in the world. She was literally a Rosie the Riveter.

Phyllis was extremely conservative and extremely ambitious—a dangerous combination. She ran for Congress twice in Illinois.

Both times she lost to her male opponents. Ever the strategic operative, and having found no success in a political realm dominated by men, Phyllis decided to join the winning team: Team Misogyny. She stopped trying to get a seat at the table by competing with men and decided to stake her claim in keeping all women out of the Constitution. She made a plan to attack the crown jewel of the women's liberation movement—the ERA—and placed herself at the center of the fight.

Only after the ERA had already passed in both houses of Congress and been ratified by many states did Phyllis start a group called STOP ERA. (S-T-O-P was an acronym for "Stop Taking Our Privileges.") She traveled around the country, giving speeches, participating in debates, and frustrating other women by saying outlandishly sexist things. She'd bait her opponents with flippant quips like, "First of all, I want to thank my husband, Fred, for letting me come—I always like to say that, because it makes the libs so mad." (Taking self-deprecating humor to new heights . . . or new lows?)

But what really made feminists mad wasn't her snide comments, it was her hypocrisy. Phyllis encouraged her STOP ERA activists to use traditional symbols of American house-wifery in their advocacy. Critics like Betty Friedan raised the fact that Phyllis herself wasn't actually a housewife like she claimed to be. In reality, she was an attorney who traveled the country full-time as an anti-ERA activist and public speaker—something not a lot of housewives got the opportunity to do. She didn't even take care of her own children; she had family and hired domestic staff to raise her six kids. In essence, Phyllis was a walking contradiction: She was living out the fruition of feminist values in private while publicly fighting against them.

Phyllis tried to convince women they would lose advantages and privileges if they were

STOP ERA

A GOOD SCAPEGOAT

Phyllis Schlafly

equal under the Constitution. She tried to frighten them into opposing their own rights. She often used violent, racially charged, and anti-gay language when talking about the horrors of the ERA. STOP ERA activists would pull dramatic stunts like dressing up in combat fatigues and drenching themselves in fake blood, parading as wounded soldiers to gruesomely (and falsely) argue that women would be dragged to the front lines of battle if the ERA passed. The Vietnam War had just ended, and many women were afraid of being drafted. She capitalized on that fear.

You've got to hand it to Phyllis. Even though she set us all back, she was a communications genius. She was acutely aware of her role as a token national female conservative spokesperson. She even wrote a book called *The Flipside of Feminism: What Conservative Women Know—and Men Can't Say*. She knew that she was the female conduit for the men's war against the ERA, and she traveled the country debating famous feminist icons like Gloria Steinem and Betty Friedan so that the men didn't have to. Phyllis Schlafly made a good scapegoat. She might have had an outsize impact, but even she insisted that she always just did the bidding of men.

It's clear she did not kill the ERA: Men did. A man added in the poison-pill deadline to the preamble of the 1972 ERA bill. A man brokered a deal to extend the deadline in 1978 to only 1982, knowing it would be too little time to remove anti-ERA state senators from office (and it would still die, despite the extra time). In every state, men held the majority of seats in state legislatures. Despite public opinion in favor of ratification, fifteen states refused to do so—men killed it one by one.

In the end, the STOP ERA was part of the success in turning the tide against the once wildly popular amendment. Former congresswoman and feminist icon Bella Abzug, who was one of Phyllis's foes, said, "Everybody's for it but we don't have it. They have allowed a highly organized minority to stop the will of a majority." But even after all her extensive groundwork building a political network of conservative women and helping to shape the new religious right as a political force, Phyllis was still denied the Cabinet position she expected in the Ronald Reagan Administration. So even after selling out her entire sex, she never got what she actually wanted: power, authority, respect—and equality.

PAT

"Equality is not debatable, we are born with it. All we are asking is for it to be recognized."

SPEARMAN

1955–Present

"I am a woman. I am African American. And I am [part] of the LGBTQ community[.] [The] discussion of equality is one I've been in all of [...] talking about special rights [...] we're talking about equal rights." She highlighted [...] largely male Congress [...] debating women's right[s] [...] the first place, "People [...] privilege always [...] not those of us who're not deserve equali[ty] [...] powerful testimony by ack[nowled]ging that the fund[amental rig]hts and dignity of [...]

CHAPTER 12

RESURRECTION

IN 2019, FOR THE first time in thirty-six years, Congress held a hearing on the Equal Rights Amendment. After the decades-long hiatus, things were on the move again in the states. For the first time since 1977, two additional states had ratified the amendment—Nevada in March of 2017 (on the heels of the Women's March!) and Illinois in May of 2018.

With Virginia as the thirty-eighth (and final necessary) state poised to ratify the amendment, the congressional hearing was a chance for all the outstanding issues to come to light in the modern era. It was a historic occasion. ERA activists from all over the country flew in for the hearing. The atmosphere was part reunion, part rock concert for constitutional law nerds. People stood in a line that snaked down the hallway waiting to get in.

Three witnesses were to speak in favor of the ERA. The representatives asked pointed, excellent questions, and the testimonies were compelling. Only one Republican even bothered to stay in the room for the entire hearing, and he mostly just ranted about his opposition to abortion and trans rights (typical). One of the witnesses was State Senator Pat Spearman, the powerhouse legislator behind the successful resurrection of the ERA in Nevada. Nevada's ratificaiton was the event that reignited the national fight that had been dormant since 1982

THE POWERHOUSE LEGISLATOR BEHIND THE SUCCESSFUL RESURRECTION OF THE ERA

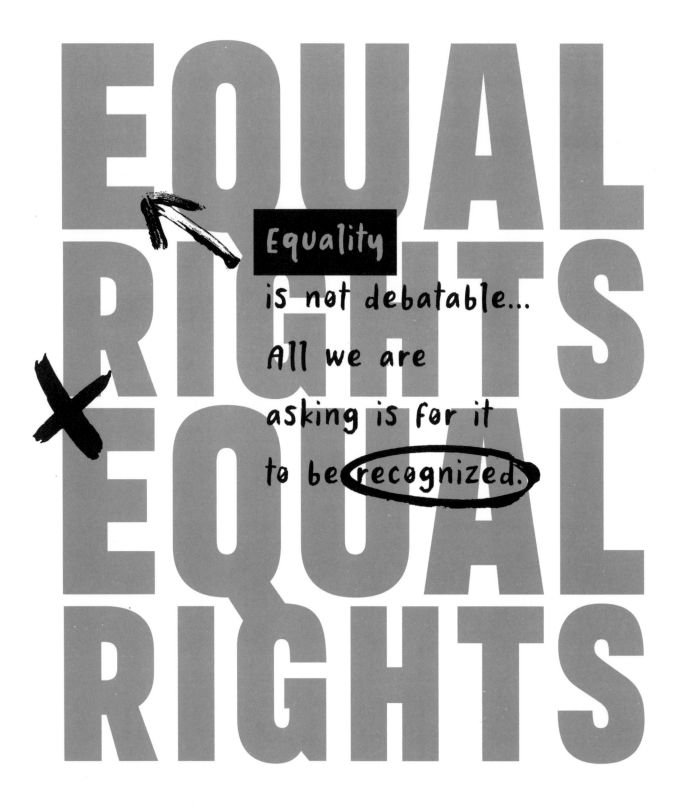

when the deadline that Barbara Jordan had helped extend expired. Senator Spearman explained that she had experienced discrimination on many levels all her life. "I am a woman. I am African American. And I am a member of the LGBTQ community. The discussion of equality is one I've been in all of my life . . . We're not talking about special rights here, we're talking about equal rights." She highlighted the absurdity of a largely male Congress even debating women's rights in the first place, "People who were born in privilege always debate whether or not those of us who were not, deserve equality." She ended her powerful testimony by acknowledging that the fundamental rights and dignity of each woman are inherent. "Equality is not debatable, we are born with it. All we are asking is for it to be recognized."

PATRICIA ANN SPEARMAN WAS born in 1955 in Indianapolis, Indiana. Her parents met when they were both part of the Wings Over Jordan Negro Chorale. In addition to being a professional singer, Pat's mother was a business school graduate and executive secretary who later felt called to ministry and became a traveling evangelist. Her dad was a veteran, Tuskegee University graduate, and electrician.

As part of the chorale, Pat's parents traveled all over the United States singing in large venues to sold-out crowds. Most of the venues where they performed did not allow Black people to go through the front door. Even the performers had to enter through the back. Local Black families often housed performers during their stops on tour because they were not allowed to stay in the hotels or eat in any of the restaurants in segregated cities. Chorale members had to make sure they ate enough to keep them going and didn't drink too much between venues so

"I am a woman. I am African American. And I am a member of the LGBTQ community. The discussion of equality is one I've been in all of my life."

The Birmingham church bombing took place the following year. Members of the Ku Klux Klan bombed a local church in a horrific act of racist violence. The explosion killed four little girls and injured many others. Once again, confused by racist hate, Pat innocently asked her mother what the girls had done to deserve it. She answered, "They went to Sunday school." Young Pat couldn't reconcile that. She said, "Why did they bomb the church?" Her mother explained they bombed the church because people were asking for the right to vote. Again, she just could not square it. "Doesn't everybody have a right to vote?" she asked, confused. Her mother replied with a simple no, an answer that would inform the course of her adult life.

they wouldn't have to stop to eat or go to the bathroom on the road, where it might have been unwelcoming or unsafe.

Things had not changed by the time Pat was a kid. In 1962, when she was seven years old, she traveled to the South for the first time. She rode the bus with her mother, passing through Pittsburgh and Columbus and traveling all the way down to Nashville. Every time the bus stopped, they stayed put for their own safety. Her mom had prepared food in advance—chicken, potato salad, and bread—but they didn't have anything to drink, so when they finally got to Nashville, Pat was dying of thirst.

As her mother was fetching their luggage, Pat ran inside, desperate to get a drink. When she opened the door, she saw a white man go up to the water fountains. One of them he drank from, and the other he snorted at and then spat in. Pat recalls how disgusted she was and how she knew she didn't want to go to that one. As she walked over to the unsullied water fountain and put her hand on it, she remembers, "My mom grabbed me from the back of my shirt. She just yanked me up so hard that I almost hit my face on the water fountain." Startled and confused, Pat kept asking her, "Why, why?" Her mother was seething. It was "the kind of anger, where her fists were clenched, her teeth clenched." She scolded her daughter, "You cannot do that! Are you trying to get killed?" Pat was confused and thought, "Killed? I just want some water."

Her mom explained to her that they were in the South now. "Do you see that sign there?" she asked. Pat said, "Yes ma'am." She was just learning to read and could only make out one of the signs. It said: White. The other sign she had to sound out phonetically. *Co-lor-ed.* "That's what we are," her mom explained.

> Instead of deterring her, the experience lit a fire within.

"We are colored and you're in the South." Pat agreed to not drink from that fountain again, but she still didn't understand what being "colored" really meant until she was much older.

The family relocated to Alabama when Pat was a teenager, and she was among the first students to integrate a high school there. She describes that horrible time, saying, "We were threatened. Some of the students, opposed to integration, threw rocks at me, and yelled the 'N' word at me every day." And the racial attacks didn't stop once Pat left Alabama to pursue her undergraduate degree at Norfolk State University in Virginia. One day, as she was walking down the road while visiting her sister in Petersburg, Virginia, a truck full of white men chased her down. They screamed racial epithets at her, and she ran for her life. She only escaped their violence by hiding in a ditch and belly-crawling to safety for half a mile. Her refusal to accept the racist treatment often led to abuse, but instead of deterring her, the experience lit a fire within. "With every physical and psychological racial attack, I became relentless to get to a place where I could make a difference."

PAT JOINED THE ROTC during college and found one of her callings in life: military service. "I was good at it," Pat noted. "It helped me with confidence." In 1977, after college graduation, Pat joined the army, just as the momentum to ratify the ERA was winding down. Many were arguing against the ERA because they claimed it would force women into military service, but Pat chose it voluntarily. She joined at a time when women weren't wanted and gay people were completely banned, but she spent twenty-nine years in the Military Police Corps of the United States Army, rising to the rank of lieutenant colonel by the time she left. She later attended the Episcopal Theological Seminary of the Southwest—the same denomination that ordained Pauli Murray (page 119)—in Austin, Texas, where she graduated with a master of divinity degree.

But Pat experienced sexism as an ordained minister, too. She'd be invited to preach at Baptist or Pentecostal churches but be slighted when she was introduced as "the speaker," rather than as "the reverend," the proper title that comes with ordination. She was often asked to stand in places other than the pulpit— subtle but unmistakable signs that a female minister wasn't as fully accepted as her male counterparts. After moving to Nevada in 2005, Spearman founded the Resurrection Faith Community Ministries, her own church in North Las Vegas where she could be the pastor. Growing up, she had preached from the pulpit on Sundays from the time she was six, so having her own church was the most natural thing in the world.

After years of getting to know her community, in 2012 Pat decided to challenge two-term incumbent Nevada Senator John Jay Lee, who opposed abortion and same-sex marriage, despite being a Democrat. Her religious upbringing and formal training are often present in the way she speaks, and almost every public address she gives is an opportunity to preach equality with the cadence of a sermon. Regardless of the topic, Pat gets people fired up and feeling the spirit, so although she only spent a fifteenth of the amount Lee had spent on the primary, she won by 26 percentage points! Pat was the first openly lesbian legislator in Nevada state history, and once in office, she created and prioritized bills that focused on things near and dear to her heart: equality, veterans, and energy. She abbreviated her platform "EVE" as a nod to the first woman of the Bible. Pat explained, "As a woman, I've experienced discrimination. Discrimination

EVERY PUBLIC ADDRESS... IS THE OPPORTUNITY TO PREACH EQUALITY WITH THE CADENCE OF A SERMON.

Pat Spearman

"WITH EVERY... RACIAL ATTACK, I BECAME RELENTLESS TO GET TO A PLACE WHERE I COULD MAKE A DIFFERENCE."

in life. Discrimination in the military. Discrimination even in church. Equality might as well be my middle name."

———

IN 2014, PAT WAS approached by a group of women who were searching for legislators to carry ERA bills in all the states that failed to ratify it in the 1970s. Helene de Boissiere-Swanson was among this group of women. (This was the same year she made her trek to Utah to visit Orrin Hatch's office from the Introduction.) Helene and several Nevadan women helped convince Spearman to take up the cause—it was an easy sell since equality was already her middle name. As soon as Pat agreed, "they went to work like Santa's elves" building support for the bill. However, it wasn't as easy to sell to other legislators as it was to Pat. The most common response was confusion: "The ERA? Isn't that already dead?" She had to explain that there had been a lull in ratifications since the 1970s, but the dream of constitutional equality was about to be resurrected in the Silver State. She assured other elected officials that only three more states were needed for ratification, and Nevada was going to be one of them.

The entire time Pat was in the armed services, she was silent about her sexuality. "I served in the US Army for twenty-nine years while in the 'closet.' I was terrified someone would out me and that would be the end of my military career." Once she left the army, she felt freer to be her authentic self. "I came out in 2009 when I was working to repeal 'Don't Ask, Don't Tell.'" But her orientation was already clear, and she said she lived in a "glass closet" since everyone could see who she really was. When Pat came out, her mother welcomed her with open arms.

Two weeks before her passing in 2002, Pat's mom told her, "Nothing is wrong with you and if anyone says something bad about you, I'll get up out of this bed and hit 'em in the name of Jesus!" It wasn't until seven years later that Pat came out of the closet. Her mother's words of acceptance were a source of strength and comfort to her. If her preacher mom could make room for her sexuality—so could everyone else.

Many of those fighting for the modern ERA are seasoned activists who never gave up on constitutional equality. One of those women is Dolores Huerta, labor leader and cofounder, along with Cesar Chavez, of United Farm Workers. In March 2021, Dolores urged all to "raise your voice and say—add ERA to the Constitution." She's among many powerful leaders from the 1970s still active in the cause.

Pat first introduced a bill to ratify the ERA in 2015, but it didn't make it out of committee—the place many bills go to die. One legislator told her she was making Nevada a "laughingstock" by introducing a relic from the past. But after the session ended, an elderly woman approached her about the ERA with tears streaming down her face. Pat described the encounter: "She's crying and she's just kind of shaking. She grabbed my hand and she said, 'Senator, I thought I wouldn't see this in my lifetime. I don't know how long I can hang on.' I said, 'Hang on, we're going to get it done.'" No state had ratified the ERA since 1977 and forty years later their chances looked slim, but Pat had made the woman a promise that she intended to keep.

Pat brought the ERA ratification up in 2015 and then again in 2016. Her introduction of the bill in 2017 followed the women's marches that had taken place all around the world. There was new momentum building behind gender equality that hadn't been seen in such large numbers since the 1970s. Determined to ride the women's wave to victory, Pat introduced the ERA ratification resolution once again. Not everyone was thrilled, of course. The opposition brought up old arguments from the 1970s: the ERA would cause women to lose benefits or force them to register for the draft. In the hearing, people threw every Chicken Little "The sky is falling!" scenario out in opposition to the ERA, but Pat persisted.

She knew that the arguments against the ERA were "not just capricious, they [were] facetious," and she committed to refuting every single one of them. She testified at the hearing wearing all white to honor the suffragists who came before her. She said, "This about equality—plain and simple. Unless all are equal, none are equal. While some would argue the time for ratifying the ERA is long past, I would respectfully disagree and argue just the opposite. . . . We still struggle with inequality under the law, and the ratification of the ERA is a step in the right direction."

When the ERA ratification bill came to the full Senate floor for a vote, Pat was nervous. "I was watching the vote tally and my heart was just racing." When the lieutenant governor announced that the ERA ratification resolution had passed, the gallery erupted. Overcome with joy, people were crying, shouting, and cheering—some reached out to strangers to hug them. Pat looked up into the gallery and locked eyes with the woman, now eighty-five years old, whom she had made a promise to two years prior. The woman looked over the balcony, wiped away her tears,

In addition to continuing the state-by-state strategy, there were women working behind the scenes on a federal fix. Political strategist Andrea Miller, who has been working on the ERA for over fifty years, initially helped her mother deliver pro-ERA flyers throughout her Chicago neighborhood when she was in junior high. She said that she thought the ERA was a "white lady issue," but her mom taught her it was just as important for them as Black women. Andrea and others came up with the plan to eliminate the deadline that was a holdover from the 1970s and started lobbying in Congress and seeking out a congressional sponsor for an ERA deadline-elimination bill. Despite most seeing it as a "lost cause," she helped secure sponsors in both the House and Senate. Just like they did in 1978, today's pro-ERA congressmembers, who include Senators Ben Cardin and Lisa. Murkowski and Representatives Carolyn Maloney and Jackie Speier are working to confirm that there can be no deadline on equality.

and waved at her, mouthing, "Thank you. Thank you." Spearman waved back and said, "We got it done. We got it done." She had accomplished what many thought was impossible. She'd gotten the ERA ratified in her state in the twenty-first century—the first in four decades.

AS A BLACK WOMAN, Pat Spearman is often faced with the question, "Isn't the ERA movement just a white women's movement?" She is adamant that it is not and that it never has been. Today, in all the states that have yet to ratify the amendment, women of color legislators are the ones leading fight. And in the past, Black suffragists like Mary Church Terrell (page 79) fought just as hard as their white contemporaries, but were thrown under the bus by them after the Nineteenth Amendment. "We have basically been ignored for a long, long time," Pat explains. "But there is a scripture in the Bible that says the stone that the builders rejected has now become the chief cornerstone"—the most important part of any building.

Pat believes "the God of the universe looks for those left out, left behind, lost people, to get the work done because we know what it feels like when we are rejected and dejected—we understand what that feels like." Looking back, she is grateful for the racism she faced as a little girl in Nashville, Tennessee. "I'm glad that it happened. I'm glad that in religious circles that I was marginalized . . . Women of color, trans women, marginalized people, God is using us because we are the stone that the folks rejected. And now, we are the chief cornerstone getting the Equal Rights Amendment ratified."

Although her leadership reignited the movement for constitutional equality and brought the push for the ERA back from the dead, Pat is always careful to insist that she didn't do it alone. "In Nevada, my name is on the bill, but behind my name are hundreds and thousands of women who worked and worked and worked to get to that moment in history, and people who held out hope long enough for me and others who supported it to get there." Pat continues to do whatever she can to make equality a reality.

"God is using us because we are the stone that the folks rejected."

DANICA ROEM

The ERA Is Queer

On the heels of the Nevada victory, Illinois ratified the bill in 2018. With only one more state needed, it was down to those with the worst record on women's rights: Alabama, Arizona, Arkansas, Florida, Georgia, Louisiana, Mississippi, Missouri, North Carolina, Oklahoma, South Carolina, Utah, and Virginia.

ERA die-hards had been working on the ground in Virginia for decades. The bill had passed in the Virginia Senate in 2011, long before most people even thought that modern-day ratifications were possible. And although the male leaders in the Virginia House of Delegates kept the ERA ratification resolution languishing in committee so it could never come up for a vote, the women of Virginia were determined to be on the right side of history.

One of the many incredible female legislators working toward ERA ratification in Virginia was Danica Roem. Danica is the first openly transgender person to serve in any US state legislature. (She beat out a thirteen-term incumbent who gave himself the title "chief homophobe.") After her big win, Danica cosponsored the resolution to ratify the ERA and served as the unofficial floor whip. She helped secure yes votes while wearing an ERA pendant necklace that her mother gave to her—a memento from her mom's own work on the ERA in the 1970s—a beautiful symbol of the unique intergenerational nature of the now century-long fight for constitutional equality.

To permanently mark the historic significance of voting to ratify the ERA in Virginia, Danica got Section 1 of the ERA tattooed on her left bicep in perfect script font: "Equality of rights under the law shall not be denied or abridged by the United States or by any State on account of sex." While the tattoo artist worked on the text of the ERA on her arm, Danica used her other hand to mark up a twenty–six–page bill coming through the subcommittee she chairs. The opposition to the ERA often tries to use trans issues to divide opponents. But thanks to the work of incredible trans women like Danica, the ERA was ratified by the thirty–eighth and final state needed, and we are one step closer to seeing the ERA inked into the US Constitution—just as it is on her arm.

As a bit of historical justice, in a 2020 case called *Bostock v. Clayton County*, the US Supreme Court decided that Title VII of the Civil Rights Act of 1964, which prohibits employment discrimination "because of . . . sex," also prohibits discrimination based on gender identity and sexual orientation. (Bet Representative Howard Smith from Virginia never saw that one coming when he wanted to sneak the word "sex" into the bill to try to kill it.) Thanks to the *Bostock* case, the ERA will also cover trans people like Danica!

Danica Roem

Equality of rights under the law shall not be denied or abridged by the United States or by any State on account of sex.

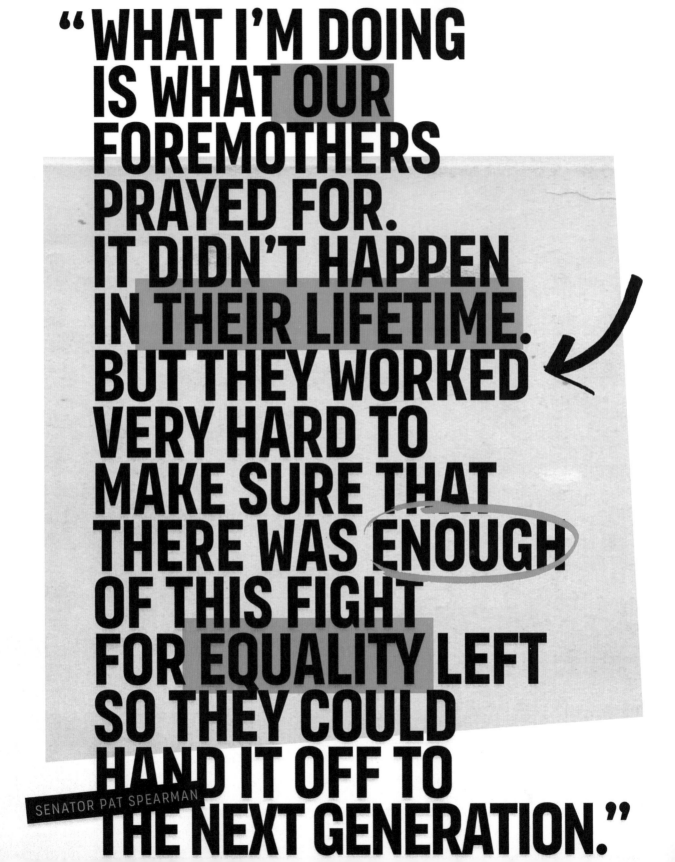

"WHAT I'M DOING IS WHAT OUR FOREMOTHERS PRAYED FOR. IT DIDN'T HAPPEN IN THEIR LIFETIME. BUT THEY WORKED VERY HARD TO MAKE SURE THAT THERE WAS ENOUGH OF THIS FIGHT FOR EQUALITY LEFT SO THEY COULD HAND IT OFF TO THE NEXT GENERATION."

SENATOR PAT SPEARMAN

CONCLUSION
FUTURE FRAMERS

WOMEN AND QUEER PEOPLE have been fighting to be included as equals in the United States since before it was founded. Native women, specifically members of the Iroquois Confederacy, participated as equals in their governance. Women contemporaries of the Founding Fathers—including their wives, like Abigail Adams—vehemently protested their inferior status and their inability to participate as equals in American politics. A more equal social system existed on the land that would become the United States thousands of years before a single colonizer or ship arrived on its shores. And, as suffragist Matilda Joslyn Gage later wrote, "When the American colonies began their resistance to English tyranny, the women—all this inherited tendency to freedom surging in their veins—were as active, earnest, determined and self-sacrificing as the men." Women fought to found this country but were then intentionally excluded from its most foundational document.

What would our Constitution have looked like if its authors reflected the diversity of the country at that time? What if there were women seated at those tables in Philadelphia? What if their female contemporary luminaries had been permitted to participate—fierce native leaders like Molly Brant, armed with

thousands of years of tradition; educated women like Mercy Otis Warren, who had seen up close the ravages of the Revolutionary War on women; and African women like Phillis Wheatley, who keenly knew the vicious abuses of chattel slavery firsthand?

What if, along the way, men had listened to women like Alice Paul, calling for not only the right to vote but also for the constitutional right to be free of all discrimination on the basis of sex? What if Congress had listened to the testimony of Pauli Murray in 1970? What if anti-equality congressmen hadn't succeeded in imposing a deadline on ratification? What if more states had ratified by the deadline Barbara Jordan and young Ruth Bader Ginsburg worked to extend?

The Framers of the Constitution acknowledged at the outset (perhaps in an uncharacteristic moment of humility) that their document may not be perfect. They wrote Article V of the Constitution, the amendment process, which left us a way to modify the document as the times changed and demanded it. The first ten amendments, known as the "Bill of Rights," are so integral to American democracy, it's hard to think they weren't included to begin with—but they weren't! Fundamental freedoms like freedom of speech, assembly, and religion were all edits made shortly after the Constitution was ratified.

Seventy years passed between the Declaration of Independence and the first convention for women's rights in America in Seneca Falls, New York, in 1848. The American women who dreamed of a more equal future in that period hardly lived to see it, but they still struggled on. They also inspired the next generation to fight not only for suffrage but also to aim higher, to seek equal opportunities for people of all genders. They didn't want us to just get the vote—they wanted us to get free.

If you are reading this book, you are part of the next generation that must work to see the ERA ratified and to fully implement its promises. Men did not give women rights, they withheld them—women today are still fixing that. It's time, as the Schuyler Sisters sing in the musical *Hamilton*, "to include women in the sequel. Work!" There is nothing more consequential or long-lasting that you can spend your time doing than trying to change the US Constitution. This fight ties us together with all the marginalized people who have come before us and with those who will come after. Senator Pat Spearman put it best when she said, "What I'm doing is what our foremothers prayed for. It didn't happen in their lifetime. But they worked very hard to make sure that there was enough of this fight for equality left, so they could hand it off to the next generation."

Once ratified, the Equal Rights Amendment will be permanent. It will be in place in one hundred years, five hundred years, and beyond—for generations and generations to come. All these women—Molly, Abigail, Phillis, Matilda, Crystal, Alice, Mary, Pauli, Martha, Patsy, Barbara, and Pat—worked and wished for us to be equal, and have our inherent rights and dignity recognized.

Add your name to that distinguished list. British suffragist Emmeline Pankhurst taught young activists like Alice Paul a helpful mantra: "Never surrender. Never give up the fight." We cannot allow one more generation to pass before we get the legal recognition we deserve in our country's blueprint. The female Framers of the US Constitution are alive today—still making history one vote, one court case, one amendment at a time. And, like the those who came before us, we know there is nothing complicated about ordinary equality.

MOLLY BRANT. NANCY WARD. ABIGAIL ADAMS. MERCY OTIS WARREN. PHILLIS WHEATLEY. BELINDA SUTTON. MATILDA JOSLYN GAGE. CRYSTAL EASTMAN. LUCY BURNS. THERE IS NOTHING COMPLICATED ABOUT ORDINARY EQUALITY.

ALICE PAUL

MARY CHURCH TERRELL. ADELINA OTERO-WARREN. ALICE PAUL. PAULI MURRAY. RUTH BADER GINSBURG. MARTHA WRIGHT GRIFFITHS. ELIZABETH HOLTZMAN. PATSY TAKEMOTO MINK. PAT SPEARMAN. BARBARA JORDAN. DANICA ROEM.

HOW YOU CAN GET INVOLVED IN RATIFYING THE ERA

FIND OUT MORE AT ORDINARYEQUALITY.COM

TELL EVERYONE ABOUT THE ERA!

CONTACT (then)

your (Federal) representative and senator— tell them they must pass the deadline-elimination bill

CONTACT

your (State) representative and senator

HAS YOUR STATE RATIFIED THE ERA?

(If so)

ASK

them to pass a #NoDeadlineOnEquality resolution urging Congress to eliminate the deadline

(If not)

CONNECT

with groups working to ratify in your state or get an ERA added to your state constitution

LISTEN

Ordinary Equality Podcast

JOIN

Generation Ratify, ERA Coalition, and Vote Equality

ACKNOWLEDGMENTS

I owe this book and my life to the women before me who lived just as they pleased and demanded that everyone else catch up to them.

I'm forever in the debt of ERA pioneers like Sonia Johnson, who sought to dismantle not only the Mormon patriarchy but also male supremacy in all its forms. Thank you, Sonia, for showing me the way to believe in yourself and your capacity so fiercely that even sexist senators cower in your presence.

Thank you to Julie Suk, who was sadly never my professor but continues to teach me about the amendment process, and who introduced the concept of seeing women as "Framers" of the constitution to me. Read her book, We the Women: The Unstoppable Mothers of the Equal Rights Amendment!

Thank you to the scholars who combed through stacks of manuscripts and original sources for years to bring us these hidden details and stories. Learning about women's history has been such a driving force in my life. We wouldn't know these women if it weren't for intrepid historians dedicated to preserving them.

Thank you to Wonder Media Network, the women-led media company that cared so much about constitutional equality that they let me make an entire podcast about it. Thanks to Jenny, Shira, Liz, Edie, Emily, Taylor, and, of course, my cohost, Jamia Wilson, for making equality sound so, so good.

Thank you to Nicole LaRue for your literal vision. You have made these pioneers come to life. Your art and wisdom are a gift.

Thank you to my parents, Donna and Jim Kelly, who taught me from day one that men and women are equal. Mom, you taught me the most important lesson I've ever learned: You don't belong to anyone else. Dad, you read to me every single night as a girl and now little girls can read my book. Thank you to my grandma Carol for being a strong, courageous woman even when it was the hardest thing in the world.

And, thank you to my partner, Jamie Manson. Your fierce heart matches mine, and your support means everything to me.
I didn't know love until I found you.

ENDNOTES

INTRODUCTION: CENTERING WOMEN IN HISTORY

XII ¶3: Bradley, Martha S. *Pedestals and Podiums: Utah Women, Religious Authority, and Equal Rights*, 333–34. Salt Lake City: Signature Books, 2005.

XV ¶1: Bradley, pg. 332.

XV ¶2: Bradley, pp. 335, 336.

XVII SIDEBAR: Gier, Nick. "Mahatma Gandhi, female activists and fasting." *Idaho State Journal*, Oct. 10, 2019. https://www.idahostatejournal.com/opinion/columns/mahatma-gandhi-female-activists-and-fasting/article_8e508ba2-19b0-52cd-ab37-45068c408376.html.

XIX ¶3: Lerner, Gerda. "Placing Women in History: Definitions and Challenges." *Feminist Studies* 3, no. 1/2 (1975): 5–14. https://doi.org/10.2307/3518951.

CHAPTER 1: MOLLY BRANT

3 ¶3: Hansen, Terri. "How the Iroquois Great Law of Peace Shaped U.S. Democracy." PBS Native America, December 17, 2018. https://www.pbs.org/native-america/blogs/native-voices/how-the-iroquois-great-law-of-peace-shaped-us-democracy; Leavey, Peggy Dymond. *Molly Brant: Mohawk Loyalist and Diplomat*, 28. Toronto: Dundurn, 2015.

4 SIDEBAR: Leavey, pg. 19.

4 ¶1: Jacobs, Renée. "Iroquois Great Law of Peace and the United States Constitution: How the Founding Fathers Ignored the Clan Mothers." *American Indian Law Review* 16, no. 2 (1991): 497.

4 ¶2: Feathers, Cynthia and Susan Feathers. "Franklin and the Iroquois Foundations of the Constitution." *The Pennsylvania Gazette*, 2007. https://www.upenn.edu/gazette/0107/gaz09.html; McKenna, Katherine M.J. "'Mary Brant (Konwatsi'tsiaienni Degonwadonti): 'Miss Molly,' Feminist Role Model or Mohawk Princess?'" Essay. In *The Human Tradition in the American Revolution*, edited by Nancy Lee Rhoden. Wilmington, DE: Rowman and Littlefield, 2000; H. Con. Res. 331, 100th Congress, 2nd Session. https://www.senate.gov/reference/resources/pdf/hconres331.pdf.

5 ¶1:   Dymond, pg. 17.

5 ¶3:   Wagner, Sally Roesch. *Sisters in Spirit: Haudenosaunee (Iroquois) Influence on Early American Feminists*, 84. Summertown, TN: Native Voices, 2001; Dymond, pg. 18.

6 SIDEBAR: O'Toole, Fintan. *White Savage: William Johnson and the Invention of America*. Albany: State University of New York Press, 2009; Moore, Lisa L., Joanna Brooks, and Caroline Wigginton. *Transatlantic Feminisms in the Age of Revolutions*, 5. Oxford: Oxford University Press, 2012.

6 ¶1:   Wagner, Sally Roesch. *The Untold Story of the Iroquois Influence on Early Feminists: Essays*. Aberdeen, SD: Sky Carrier Press, 1996; Fletcher, Alice Cunningham. "The Legal Conditions of Indian Women." Speech, National Woman Suffrage Association Evening Session, Washington, DC, March 29, 1888.

7 SIDEBAR: Deer, Sarah. *The Beginning and End of Rape: Confronting Sexual Violence in Native America*. Minneapolis: University of Minnesota Press, 2015; Wagner, Sally Roesch. "The Iroquois Confederacy: A Native American Model for Non-sexist Men," *Changing Men* vol. 19, Spring/Summer (1988): 32–34; Wagner, *Sisters*, pg. 68.

7 ¶1:   O'Toole, *White Savage*; Dymond, pg. 39.

7 ¶2:   O'Toole, *White Savage*.

9 ¶1:   Dymond, pg. 51; McKenna, pg. 192.

9 ¶2:   Dymond, pp. 87, 71, 102.

11 ¶3:   Moore, pg. 4.

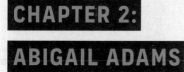

CHAPTER 2:
ABIGAIL ADAMS

13 ¶1:   Holton, Woody. *Abigail Adams: A Life*, 7. New York: Atria Books, 2010; Coe, Alexis. "Abigail Adams Persisted." *Lenny Letter*, December 12, 2017. https://www.lennyletter.com/story/abigail-adams-defends-black-servant.

13 ¶2:   Moore, Lisa L., Joanna Brooks, and Caroline Wigginton. *Transatlantic Feminisms in the Age of Revolutions*, 168. Oxford: Oxford University Press, 2012.

15 ¶2:   Moore, pg. 164; Holton, pg. 25.

15 ¶3:   Daher, Danniah. "5 First Ladies Who Are Cooler Than Their Husbands." *BUST*, n.d. https://bust.com/feminism/15632-five-first-ladies-who-are-cooler-than-their-husands.html.

16 SIDEBAR: Adams, Abigail. Letter to John Adams. *Adams Family Papers*. Massachusetts Historical Society, March 31–April 5, 1776. https://www.masshist.org/digitaladams/archive/doc?id=L17760331aa.

16 ¶1:   Coe, "Abigail Adams Persisted."

18 ¶1:   Moore, pg. 167.

18 ¶2:   Holton, pp. 67, 86.

18 ¶3:   Adams, Abigail. Letter to John Adams. *Adams Family Papers*. Massachusetts Historical Society, September 22, 1774. https://www.masshist.org/digitaladams/archive/doc?id=L17740922aa; Wagner, Sally Roesch. "The Iroquois Confederacy: A Native American Model for Non-sexist Men," Changing Men vol. 19, Spring/Summer (1988): 39.

19 SIDEBAR: Schuessler, Jennifer. "On the Trail of America's First Women to Vote." *The New York Times*, February 24, 2020. https://www.nytimes.com/2020/02/24/arts/first-women-voters-new-jersey.html.

19 ¶1:   Adams, Abigail. Letter to John Adams. *Adams Family Papers*. Massachusetts Historical Society, July 13, 1776. https://www.masshist.org/publications/adams-papers/view?id=ADMS-04-02-02-0026#AFC02d026n8; Wagner, "The Iroquois Confederacy," pg. 39.

20 ¶1:   Holton, pp. 9, 15; Watson, Robert P. "The 'White Glove Pulpit': A History of Policy Influence by First Ladies." OAH *Magazine of History* 15, no. 3 (2001): 9–14.

20 ¶2:   Holton, pg. ix.

21 SIDEBAR: Michals, Debra. "Deborah Sampson (1760–1827)." National Women's History Museum, 2015.

https://www.womenshistory.org/education-resources/biographies/deborah-sampson; Adams, Letter to John Adams. March 31–April 5, 1776; Moore, pg. 174.

23 ¶1: Warren, Mercy Otis. *History of the Rise, Progress, and Termination of the American Revolution.* 1805.

CHAPTER 3:
PHILLIS WHEATLEY

25 ¶2: O'Neale, Sondra A. "Phillis Wheatley." Poetry Foundation, n.d. https://www.poetryfoundation.org/poets/phillis-wheatley; "Today in History, September 1: Phillis Wheatley." The Library of Congress, n.d. https://www.loc.gov/item/today-in-history/september-01/; "Selina Hastings, Countess of Huntingdon, Letters and Images." Bridwell Library, Southern Methodist University, n.d. https://www.smu.edu/libraries/digitalcollections/hunt; "Wheatley, Susanna." Dartmouth University, n.d. https://collections.dartmouth.edu/occom/html/ctx/personography/pers0574.ocp.html.

25 ¶3: Moore, Lisa L., Joanna Brooks, and Caroline Wigginton. *Transatlantic Feminisms in the Age of Revolutions,* 146. Oxford: Oxford University Press, 2012.

27 ¶1: Holton, Woody. *Abigail Adams: A Life,* 71. New York: Atria Books, 2010.

27 ¶2: Kelly, Kate and Jamia Wilson. "Remember the Ladies." Ordinary Equality. Podcast audio. https://podcasts.apple.com/us/podcast/remember-the-ladies/id1492330633?i=1000463241037.

28 ¶1: O'Neale, "Phillis Wheatley."

29 ¶1: Caretta, Vincent. *Phillis Wheatley: Biography of a Genius in Bondage.* Athens, GA: University of Georgia Press, 2011; "Today in History, September 1: Phillis Wheatley"; Moore, pg. 29; Sancho, Ignatius. *Letters of the Late Ignatius Sancho, an African,* 112. Edited by Vincent Caretta. Peterborough, Canada: Broadview Press, 2015.

30 SIDEBAR: "Phillis Wheatley." Biography.com, January 11, 2021. https://www.biography.com/writer/phillis-wheatley.

30 ¶1: Biography.com, "Phillis Wheatley."

30 ¶2: O'Neale, "Phillis Wheatley"; Michals, Debra. "Phillis Wheatley (1753–1784)." National Women's History Museum, 2015. https://www.womenshistory.org/education-resources/biographies/phillis-wheatley.

31 SIDEBAR: Michals, "Phillis Wheatley."

31 ¶1: O'Neale, "Phillis Wheatley."

31 ¶2: Woodlief, Ann. "On Phillis Wheatley." Virginia Commonwealth University. https://archive.vcu.edu/english/engweb/webtexts/Wheatley/philbio.htm.

33 ¶1: Wheatley, Phillis. Letter from Phillis Wheatley to Dear Obour. Library of Congress, March 21, 1774. https://www.loc.gov/resource/rbpe.0370260b.

34 SIDEBAR: Moore, pg. 13.

34 ¶2: "Today in History, September 1: Phillis Wheatley"; O'Neale, "Phillis Wheatley"; "Today in History, September 1: Phillis Wheatley."

35 ¶1: Wheatley, Phillis. "An elegiac poem, on the death of that celebrated divine, and eminent servant of Jesus Christ, the Reverend and learned George Whitefield, chaplain to the Right Honourable the Countess of Huntington." Library of Congress, n.d. https://www.loc.gov/item/06020401.

37 ¶1: Moore, pg. 186.

37 ¶2: Moore, pp. 186, 188; "Belinda Sutton and Her Petitions." Royall House & Slave Quarters, n.d. https://royallhouse.org/slavery/belinda-sutton-and-her-petitions.

37 ¶3: Royall House, "Belinda Sutton."

CHAPTER 4:
MATILDA JOSLYN GAGE

39 ¶1: Wagner, Sally Roesch. "That Word Is Liberty: A Biography of Matilda Joslyn Gage," 52–53. PhD dissertation, University of California, Santa Cruz

(1978); Carpenter, Angelica Shirley. *Born Criminal: Matilda Joslyn Gage, Radical Suffragist*, 17. Pierre, SD: South Dakota Historical Society Press, 2018; Gage, Matilda Joslyn. Speech in "Report of the International Council of Women, Assembled by the National Woman Suffrage Association, Washington, DC, March 25 to April 1, 1888" (Washington, DC: Rufus H. Darby, 1888), 1:347.

39 ¶2: Gage, Matilda Joslyn. *Woman, Church and State*, 20. Amherst, New York: Humanity Books, 2002.

41 ¶1: Carpenter, *Born Criminal*, pp. 12, 15.

41 ¶3: Carpenter, *Born Criminal*, pp. 29, 31

42 ¶1: Wagner, Sally Roesch. "Matilda Joslyn Gage Enters the Women's Rights Movement 1852." The Matilda Joslyn Gage Foundation, 2019.

42 ¶2: Corey, Mary E. *The Political Life and Times of Matilda Joslyn Gage*, 10–11. Rochester, NY: Paramount Market Publishing, 2019; Wagner, "Matilda Joslyn Gage Enters the Women's Rights Movement," pg. 14.

43 SIDEBAR: Resnick, Brian. "Nettie Stevens discovered XY sex chromosomes. She didn't get credit because she had two X's." Vox, July 7, 2017. https://www.vox.com/2016/7/7/12105830/ nettie-stevens-genetics-gender-sex-chromosomes.

45 ¶1: Gage, *Woman Church and State*, pg. 5; Carpenter, *Born Criminal*, pg. 190.; Corey, pg. 15.

45 ¶2: Rivette, Barbara S. "Fayetteville's First Woman Voter," *Matilda Joslyn Gage Reader Series*, ii, 6. Fayetteville, NY: Matilda Joslyn Gage Foundation, 2006.

47 ¶1: Corey, pg. 15.

47 ¶2: Carpenter, Angelica Shirley. *The Voice of Liberty*, 7, 13, 19. Pierre, SD: South Dakota Historical Society Press, 2020.

48 ¶1: Gage, Matilda Joslyn. "Prospectus," *The National Citizen and Ballot Box* vol. 3, no. 2. (1878): 1; Corey, pp. 19, 52.

48 ¶2: Gage, *Woman Church and State*, pg. 16.

49 SIDEBAR: Wagner, Sally Roesch. *We Want Equal Rights!: How Suffragists Were Influenced by Haudenosaunee Women*, 21. Summertown, TN: 7th Generation, 2020.

49 ¶1: Corey, pg. 121.

50 ¶1: Carpenter, *Born Criminal*, pg. 177; Corey, pg. 108.

52 SIDEBAR: Gage, Matilda Joslyn. "Public Defenders." *Liberal Thinker*, January 1890.

50 ¶2: Matilda Joslyn Gage Foundation. "A Woman's Right to Her Body and Her Life." *The Matilda Joslyn Gage Reader Series*, 3; Carpenter, *Born Criminal*, pg. 188.

51 ¶1: Corey, pg. 67.

51 ¶2: Corey, pg. 42.

54 ¶1: Wagner, Sally Roesch. "The Wonderful Mother of Oz." *Matilda Joslyn Gage Reader Series*, 9. Fayetteville, NY: The Matilda Joslyn Gage Foundation, 2003.

54 ¶2: Dean, Michelle. "What 'Oz' Owes to Early Radical Feminism." The Nation, March 8, 2013. https://www.thenation.com/article/archive/ what-oz-owes-early-radical-feminism.

54 ¶3: Wagner, "The Wonderful Mother of Oz," pp. 10, 11; Carpenter, *Born Criminal*, pg. 212.

CHAPTER 5:
CRYSTAL EASTMAN

57 ¶1: Herman, Susan N. "Crystal Eastman, the ACLU's Underappreciated Founding Mother." ACLU, July 12, 2019. https://www.aclu.org/issues/free-speech/ crystal-eastman-aclus-underappreciated-founding- mother.

57 ¶2: Law, Sylvia A. "Crystal Eastman: NYU Law Graduate." *New York University Law Review*, Vol. 66. (December 1991): 1967; Cook, Blanche Wiesen. *Crystal Eastman on Women and Revolution*, 44. New York: Oxford University Press, 1978.

59 ¶1: Law, "NYU Law Graduate," pp. 1968, 1969

59 ¶2: Law, "NYU Law Graduate," pp. 1969; Cook, pg. 3.

60 ¶1: Cook, pp. 4, 9; Aronson, Amy. *Crystal Eastman: A Revolutionary Life*, 43. New York: Oxford University Press, 2020.

60 SIDEBAR: Cook, pg. 44; Law, "NYU Law Graduate," pg. 1970.

60 ¶2: Cook, pp. 4, 43.

62 ¶1: Law, "NYU Law Graduate," pg. 1966.

63 ¶2: Aronson, pg. 58; Eastman, Crystal. Letter to Annis Eastman. Schlesinger Library, Radcliffe College. Crystal Eastman collection, Box 6, Folder 169, June 25, 1907.

63 ¶1: Law, "NYU Law Graduate," pg. 1981; Cook, pg. 6.

63 ¶2: Cook, pg. 27.

63 ¶3: Herman, Susan N. "Crystal Eastman, the ACLU's Underappreciated Founding Mother." ACLU, July 12, 2019. https://www.aclu.org/issues/free-speech/crystal-eastman-aclus-underappreciated-founding-mother.

64 ¶1: Law, Sylvia A. "Crystal Eastman." *Pace Law Review*, Vol. 12, Issue 3. (Fall 1992): 536; Law, Sylvia A. "Crystal Eastman: Organizer for Women's Rights, Peace, and Civil Liberties in the 1910s," Valparaiso University Law Review, vol. 28. (1994): 1308.

64 ¶3: Law, "Organizer for Women's Rights," pg. 1314.

65 ¶1: Aronson, pp. 98, 106.

66 ¶1: Aronson, pg. 111; Herman, "Crystal Eastman."

66 ¶2: Law, "Organizer for Women's Rights," pg. 1317; Cook, pg. 65.

67 ¶1: Cook, pg. 60.

68 ¶2: Lapidus, Lenora M. and Cristel Taveras. "The Women Behind the 19th Amendment Had a Grander Vision Than Just the Right to Vote." ACLU, August 30, 2016. https://www.aclu.org/blog/womens-rights/women-behind-19th-amendment-had-grander-vision-just-right-vote.

68 ¶3: Cook, pg. 161.

68 ¶1: Cook, pp. 30, 157.

71 ¶2: Law, "Crystal Eastman," pg. 538; Cook, pg. 16.

71 ¶3: Cook, pg. 20.

71 ¶3: ACLU. "Crystal Eastman." https://www.aclu.org/other/crystal-eastman; Law, "Crystal Eastman," pg. 538.

72 SIDEBAR: McKay, Claude. *A Long Way from Home*, 122. Boston: Mariner Books, 1970.

72 ¶2: ACLU, "Crystal Eastman"; Aronson, pp. 179, 180.

73 SIDEBAR: Herman, "Crystal Eastman."

73 ¶1: Aronson, pp. xx, 218; Eastman, Crystal. "Birth Control in the Feminist Program." *The Birth Control Review*, January 1918. Reprinted in *Crystal Eastman on Women and Revolution* by Blanche Wiesen Cook. New York: Oxford University Press, 1978.

74 ¶1: Aronson, pg. 252; Cook, pp. 34, 373; Simkin, John, "Crystal Eastman." Spartacus Educational, n.d. https://spartacus-educational.com/USAWeastman.htm.

76 ¶1: Cassidy, Tina. *Mr. President, How Long Must We Wait? Alice Paul, Woodrow Wilson and the Fight for the Right to Vote*, 198. New York: 37 Ink, 2019; Aronson, pg. 48.

76 ¶3: "Lucy Burns (1879–1966)." Turning Point Suffrage Memorial. https://suffragistmemorial.org/lucy-burns-1879-1966.

CHAPTER 6:
MARY CHURCH TERRELL

78: Parker, Alison M. "A Colored Woman in a White World": The Intersectional Perspective of Mary Church Terrell." American Historical Association, January 5, 2015. https://aha.confex.com/aha/2015/webprogram/Paper15812.html.

79 ¶2: Cooper, Brittney C. *Beyond Respectability: The Intellectual Thought of Race Women*, 74. Chicago: University of Illinois Press, 2017.

81 ¶1: Mansky, Jackie. "How One Woman Helped End Lunch Counter Segregation in the Nation's Capital." *Smithsonian Magazine*, June 8, 2016. https://www.smithsonianmag.com/history/how-one-woman-helped-end-lunch-counter-segregation-nations-capital-180959345/; Watson, E. "Robert Reed Church, Sr. (1839-1912)." BlackPast.org, November 192007. https://www.blackpast.org/African-american-history/Robert-reed-church-sr-1839-1912/.

81 ¶3: Cooper, pg. 70.

82 SIDEBAR: "A Day in History, May 1–3, 1866: Memphis Massacre," Zinn Education Project. https://www.zinnedproject.org/news/tdih/1866-memphis-riots.

82 ¶1: Wilks, Jennifer M. "The French and Swiss Diaries of Mary Church Terrell, 1888–89." *Palimpsest: A Journal on Women, Gender, and the Black International,* Volume 3, Issue 1 (2014).

82 ¶3: Jones, Martha S. *Vanguard: How Black Women Broke Barriers, Won the Vote, and Insisted on Equality for All,* 155. New York: Basic Books, 2020; Michals, Debra. "Mary Church Terrell: 1863–1954." National Women's History Museum, n.d. https://www.womenshistory.org/education-resources/biographies/mary-church-terrell; Wilks, "Diaries."

83 ¶1: Wilks, "Diaries"; Michals, "Mary Church Terrell."

85 ¶1: Parker, "Black Suffragist"; Terrell, Mary Church. "Testimony Before the House Judiciary Committee on the Equal Rights Amendment, March 10, 1948." Speech. Iowa State University Archives of Women's Political Communication. https://awpc.cattcenter.iastate.edu/2017/03/21/testimony-before-the-house-judiciary-committee-on-the-equal-rights-amendment-march-10-1948/.

85 ¶2: Parker, "Black Suffragist."

86 ¶1: Cooper, pp. 70, 71; Jones, pg. 155.

86 ¶14: "The People's Grocery . . . and Ida B. Wells." Historic Memphis, n.d. http://historic-memphis.com/biographies/peoples-grocery/peoples-grocery.html.

87 ¶1: "The People's Grocery Lynchings (Thomas Moss, Will Stewart, Calvin McDowell)." Lynching Sites Project, n.d. https://lynchingsitesmem.org/lynching/peoples-grocery-lynchings-thomas-moss-will-stewart-calvin-mcdowell.

87 ¶3: "Mary Church Terrell (1863–1954): Educator, Writer, Civil Rights Activist." VCU Libraries Social Welfare History Project, n.d. https://socialwelfare.library.vcu.edu/eras/terrell-mary-church; Gailani, Matthew. "'Lifting as We Climb' Mary Church Terrell and the 19th Amendment." Tennessee State Museum, August 11, 2020. https://tnmuseum.org/junior-curators/posts/lifting-as-we-climb-mary-church-terrell-and-the-19th-amendment.

88 ¶1: Michals, "Mary Church Terrell"; "Black History Makers 1865–1914." *Los Angeles Sentinel,* n.d. https://lasentinel.net/black-history-makers-1865-1914.html/18.

88 ¶12: Parker, "Black Suffragist."

89 ¶1: Parker, "Black Suffragist."

89 ¶2: Terrell, "Testimony Before the House Judiciary Committee"; Terrell, Mary Church. Mary Church Terrell Papers: Speeches and Writings, 1866–1953. "Why We Need the Equal Rights Amendment." Library of Congress. https://www.loc.gov/resource/mss42549.mss42549-024_00126_00128/?r=-0.218,-0.047,1.435,0.95,0.

91 ¶1: Terrell, "Why We Need the Equal Rights Amendment."

91 ¶2: Cooper, pg. 75.

91 ¶3: Quigley, Joan. "How D.C. Ended Segregation a Year Before Brown v. Board of Education." *Washington Post,* January 15, 2016; Mansky, "One Woman."

92 ¶2: Quigley, "How D.C. Ended Segregation"; Mansky, "One Woman."

94 ¶2: Machen, Meredith. "Nina Otero-Warren: New Mexico Suffragist." League of Women Voters New Mexico, n.d. https://www.lwvcnm.org/two-centennials/lwv-bios/nina-otero-warren/.

94 ¶3: Ybarra, Priscilla Solis. "Who was Nina Otero Warren." Nina Otero Community, n.d. https://ninaotero.sfps.info/about_us/who_was_nina_otero_warren; Brandman, Mariana. "Adelina Otero-Warren: 1881–1965." National Women's History Museum, n.d. https://www.womenshistory.org/education-resources/biographies/adelina-otero-warren.

95 ¶1: Machen, "New Mexico Suffragist."

95 ¶3: Morningstar. Amadea. "Charlotte Whaley: Nina Otero-Warren of Santa Fe." *The Santa Fe New Mexican,* August 20, 1995. https://www.newspapers.com/clip/14467055/nina-otero-warren-of-santa-feby; "LGBTQ Homesteaders." National Park Service, n.d. https://www.nps.gov/home/learn/historyculture/lgbtq-homesteaders.htm; "What Is the Las Dos Homestead?" Las Dos Homestead, n.d. https://www.lasdoshomestead.com/lasdoshistory.

CHAPTER 7: ALICE PAUL

97 ¶1: Kops, Deborah. *Alice Paul and the Fight for Women's Rights: From the Vote to the Equal Rights Amendment*, 41. New York: Calkins Creek, 2017; DeWolf, Rebecca. *Gendered Citizenship: The Original Conflict over the Equal Rights Amendment, 1920–1963*, 46. Lincoln, Nebraska: University of Nebraska Press, 2021.

99 ¶2: Levering, Patricia W. "Mothers of Feminism: The Story of Quaker Women in by Margaret Hope Bacon." *Los Angeles Times*, September 28, 1986. https://www.latimes.com/archives/la-xpm-1986-09-28-bk-9604-story.html.

99 ¶3: Zahniser, J.D. and Amelia R. Fry. *Alice Paul Claiming Power*, 13, 19. New York: Oxford University Press, 2014.

100 SIDEBAR: Cassidy, Tina. *Mr. President, How Long Must We Wait? Alice Paul, Woodrow Wilson and the Fight for the Right to Vote*, 6–7. New York: 37 Ink, 2019.

101 ¶1: Kops, pp. 22, 26.

102 ¶1: Cassidy, pp. 13, 14, 198.

102 ¶2: Cassidy, pg. 16; Kops, pg. 35.

104 ¶1: Kops, pg. 44.

104 ¶2: Kops, pg. 45.

104 ¶3: Kops, pg. 50.

107 ¶2: Kops, pg. 74.

107 ¶3: Kops, pg. 79.

107 ¶4: Kops, pp. 125, 135.

108 ¶1: Kops, pg. 35.

109 SIDEBAR: Kops, pg. 107; Cassidy, pg. 189.

109 ¶1: Kops, pg. 135.

110 SIDEBAR: Rupp, Leila J. and Verta Taylor. *Survival in the Doldrums: The American Women's Rights Movement, 1945 to the 1960s*, 40. New York: Oxford University Press, 1987.

110 ¶1: Cook, Blanche Wiesen. *Crystal Eastman on Women and Revolution*, 61. New York: Oxford University Press, 1978; Kops, pg. 139.

110 ¶2: Cassidy, pg. 245.

111 ¶1: Kops, pg. 140; Cassidy, pg. 91.

111 ¶2: DeWolf, pg. 50.

112 SIDEBAR: Kops, pg. 145.

112 ¶1: Kops, pg. 142; Rupp and Taylor, pg. 36; DeWolf, pg. 81.

112 ¶2: Rupp and Taylor, pg. 17; Aronson, Amy. *Crystal Eastman: A Revolutionary Life*, 242. New York: Oxford University Press, 2020; Kops, pg. 155.

113 ¶1: Cassidy, pg. 254.

113 ¶2: Menand, Louis. "How Women Got in on the Civil Rights Act." *The New Yorker*, July 14, 2014. https://www.newyorker.com/magazine/2014/07/21/sex-amendment.

114 SIDEBAR: Sandomir, Richard. "Aileen Hernandez, 90, Ex-NOW President and Trailblazer, Dies," February 28, 2014. https://www.nytimes.com/2017/02/28/us/aileen-hernandez-dead-womens-rights-champion.html.

117 ¶1: Guha, Ramachandra. "How the Suffragettes Influenced Mahatma Gandhi." *Hindustan Times*, February 24, 2018. https://www.hindustantimes.com/columns/how-the-suffragettes-influenced-mahatma-gandhi/story-d64CKd7REk1AF41JQdUtfN.html.

117 ¶2: Gier, Nick. "Mahatma Gandhi, female activists and fasting." *Idaho State Journal*, Oct. 10, 2019. https://www.idahostatejournal.com/opinion/columns/mahatma-gandhi-female-activists-and-fasting/article_8e508ba2-19b0-52cd-ab37-45068c408376.html; Cassidy, pg. 16.

CHAPTER 8: PAULI MURRAY

119 SIDEBAR: Simmons-Thorne, Naomi. "Pauli Murray and the Pronominal Problem: a De-essentialist Trans Historiography." *The Activist History Review*, May

30, 2019. https://activisthistory.com/2019/05/30/
pauli-murray-and-the-pronominal-problem-a-
de-essentialist-trans-historiography; Rosenberg,
Rosalind. *Jane Crow: The Life of Pauli Murray*, 57–60.
New York: Oxford University Press, 2017; "Who Is
Pauli Murray?" Pauli Murray Center for History and
Social Justice, 2014. https://www.paulimurraycenter.
com/who-is-pauli.

119 ¶1: "Pauli Murray." Americans Who Tell the Truth,
n.d. https://www.americanswhotellthetruth.org/
portraits/pauli-murray.

119 ¶2: Rosenberg, pg. 64.

121 ¶1: "Interview with Pauli Murray." Southern Oral
History Program Collection, February 13, 1976.
https://docsouth.unc.edu/sohp/html_use/
G-0044.html.

121 ¶2: Pauli Murray Center, "Who Is Pauli Murray?";
Schulz, Kathryn. "The Many Lives of Pauli
Murray." *The New Yorker*, April 10, 2017. https://
www.newyorker.com/magazine/2017/04/17/
the-many-lives-of-pauli-murray.

121 ¶3: "An Exhibit About the Life and Legacy of
20th-Century Human Rights Champion Pauli
Murray." Duke University, 2021. https://sites.
fhi.duke.edu/paulimurrayproject/identity-map;
Rosenberg, pg. 20; Schulz, "Many Lives"; Bell-Scott,
Patricia. *The Firebrand and the First Lady*, 14. New
York: Vintage Books, 2016; Mayeri, Serena. "Pauli
Murray and the Twentieth-Century Quest for Legal
and Social Equality." *Indiana Journal of Law and
Social Equality* 2, no. 1. (2014) https://scholarship.
law.upenn.edu/faculty_scholarship/1530.

122 SIDEBAR: Murray, Pauli. *Proud Shoes: The Story of an
American Family*. Boston: Beacon Press, 1999.

124 SIDEBAR: Strum, Philippa. "Pauli Murray's Indelible
Mark on the Fight for Equal Rights." American
Civil Liberties Union, June 24, 2020. https://
www.aclu.org/issues/womens-rights/
pauli-murrays-indelible-mark-fight-equal-rights.

124 ¶1: Rosenberg, pp. 29, 30.

124 ¶2: Rosenberg, pg. 36.

125 ¶1: Bell-Scott, pp. 13, 56; Rosenberg, pg. 56.

125 ¶2: Rosenberg, pg. 22; Bell-Scott, pg. 39; Strum, "Pauli
Murray's Indelible Mark."

125 ¶3: Bell-Scott, pg. 39; Murray, Pauli. Correspondence
with Eleanor Roosevelt and FDR. ACLU, 1938.
https://www.aclu.org/letter/pauli-murray-
correspondence-eleanor-roosevelt-and-fdr.

126 ¶1: Murray, Correspondence with Eleanor Roosevelt
and FDR.

126 ¶2: Bell-Scott, pg. 100.

127 SIDEBAR: Golay, Michael. *America 1933: The Great
Depression, Lorena Hickok, Eleanor Roosevelt, and
the Shaping of the New Deal*, 190. New York: Simon &
Schuster, 2016.

127 ¶2: Bell-Scott, pg. 110; Rosenberg, pg. 117; Strum, "Pauli
Murray's Indelible Mark."

128 ¶1: Strum, "Pauli Murray's Indelible Mark."

128 ¶2: Bell-Scott, pg. 134.

128 ¶3: Bell-Scott, pg. 133; Strum, "Pauli Murray's Indelible
Mark"; Lu, Tina. "LU: Pauli Murray, In the Now."
Yale Daily News, September 5, 2017. https://
yaledailynews.com/blog/2017/09/05/lu-pauli-
murray-in-the-now; Schulz, "Many Lives."

130 ¶2: Schulz, "Many Lives."

131 ¶1: Murray, Pauli. "The Negro Woman in the Quest for
Equality." Speech presented at the National Council
of Negro Women. Washington, DC, November 14,
1963. https://cpb-us-e1.wpmucdn.com/blogs.
uoregon.edu/dist/7/11428/files/2017/03/Murray-
The-Negro-Woman-2clsq0g.pdf.

131 ¶2: Rosenberg, pg. 299.

132 SIDEBAR: Murray, Pauli and Dorothy Kenyon. Telegram.
ACLU, September 23, 1970. https://www.aclu.org/
other/pauli-murray-and-dorothy-kenyon-
telegram-september-1970.

133 ¶1: Murray, Pauli. Hearings on S. J. Res. 61 and S.J. Res.
231 Before the S. Comm. on the Judiciary, 91st Cong.
427–33 (1970).

133 ¶2: Murray, Pauli. "The Negro Woman's Stake in the
Equal Rights Amendment." *Harvard Civil Rights-
Civil Liberties Law Review* 6, no. 2 (March 1971): 253,
254, and 259.

134 ¶3: Bell-Scott, pg. 344.

134 SIDEBAR: Bell-Scott, pg. 359; "An Exhibit." Duke
University, 2021.

135 ¶1: "Pauli Murray Hall: UNC's Departments of History, Political Science, and Sociology and the Curriculum on Peace, War, and Defense begin the renaming of Hamilton Hall." UNC College of Arts and Sciences: History. https://history.unc.edu/2020/07/pauli-murray-hall-uncs-departments-of-history-political-science-and-sociology-and-the-curriculum-on-peace-war-and-defense-begin-the-renaming-of-hamilton-hall.

136 ¶2: Ginsburg, Ruth Bader. "The Need for the Equal Rights Amendment." *American Bar Association Journal* vol. 59, no. 9 (September 1973); Ginsburg, Ruth Bader. "The Equal Rights Amendment is the Way." *Harvard Women's Law Journal.* vol. 1, no. 19 (1978); Ginsburg, Ruth Bader. Hearings Before the Subcommittee on Civil and Constitutional Rights of the Judiciary Committee, U.S. House of Representatives, 95th Congress, H.J. Res 638, May 1978; Eisner, Jane. "Jane Eisner Interviews Ruth Bader Ginsburg: Transcript." *Forward*, February 5, 2018. https://forward.com/opinion/393687/jane-eisner-interviews-ruth-bader-Ginsburg-transcript.

137 ¶1: Schwab, Nikki. "Ginsburg: Make ERA Part of the Constitution." *U.S. News & World Report*, April 18, 2014. https://www.usnews.com/news/blogs/washington-whispers/2014/04/18/justice-Ginsburg-make-equal-rights-amendment-part-of-the-constitution.

137 ¶2: Moyers, Bill. "Transcript: Justice Ruth Bader Ginsburg in Conversation with Bill Moyers." BillMoyers.com, February 14, 2020. https://billmoyers.com/story/transcript-justice-ruth-bader-Ginsburg-in-conversation-with-bill-moyers.

CHAPTER 9: MARTHA GRIFFITHS WRIGHT

138: "Martha Griffiths." Michigan Supreme Court Historical Society, n.d. http://www.micourthistory.org/women-and-the-law/martha-griffiths.

139 ¶1: "Griffiths, Martha Wright 1912–2003." United States House of Representatives History, Art & Archives, n.d. https://history.house.gov/People/Detail/14160.

139 ¶3: United States House of Representatives, "Griffiths"; Jackson, Harold. "Martha Griffiths." *The Guardian*, April 28, 2003. https://www.theguardian.com/news/2003/apr/29/guardianobituaries.haroldjackson.

141 ¶1: Crass, Scott. "Martha Griffiths: Mother of ERA and Title VII." The Moderate Voice, July 6, 2013. https://themoderatevoice.com/martha-griffithsmother-of-era-and-title-vii.

141 ¶2: Jackson, "Martha Griffiths"; Saxon, Wolfgang. "Martha Griffiths, 91, Dies; Fighter for Women's Rights." *The New York Times*, April 25, 2003. https://www.nytimes.com/2003/04/25/us/martha-griffiths-91-dies-fighter-for-women-s-rights.html.

142 ¶1: United States House of Representatives, "Griffiths"; Thomas, Gillian. "This Women's History Month, Celebrate Title VII for Banning Sex Discrimination in the Workplace." ACLU, March 9, 2016. https://www.aclu.org/blog/womens-rights/womens-rights-workplace/womens-history-month-celebrate-title-vii-banning-sex.

143 SIDEBAR: United States House of Representatives, "Griffiths"; Jackson, "Martha Griffiths."

142 ¶1: Kyvig, David E. *Explicit and Authentic Acts: Amending the U.S. Constitution, 1776–1995*, 402–403. Lawrence, KS: University Press of Kansas, 1996.

143 ¶2: Foerstel, Karen. *Biographical Dictionary of Congressional Women*, 109–110. Westport, CT: Greenwood Press, 1999; Holland, Jesse J. "5 Things to Know About the 1964 Civil Rights Act." *The St. Augustine Record*, July 2, 2014. https://www.staugustine.com/article/20140702/NEWS/307029959.

144 ¶1: "Martha Griffiths and the Equal Rights Amendment." National Archives, n.d. https://www.archives.gov/legislative/features/griffiths.

145 ¶1: Griffiths, Martha Wright. Oral History Interview. Congressional Record, House, 91st Cong., 2nd sess. (August 10, 1970): 28005; USAFMOC: 82–83; Suk, Julie. *We the Women: The Unstoppable Mothers of the Equal Rights Amendment*, 79. New York: Skyhorse Publishing, 2020.

145 ¶2: Griffiths, Oral History Interview. 28004–28005.

145 ¶3: National Archives, "Martha Griffiths"; Suk, 61; Jackson, "Martha Griffiths."

147 SIDEBAR: Chamberlin, Hope. *A Minority of Members: Women in the U.S. Congress*, 260. New York: Praeger Publishers, 1973.

149 ¶1: Saxon, "Martha Griffiths."

149 ¶2: Saxon, "Martha Griffiths"; Alessandra Stanley, "The 1990 Elections; The 1990 Campaign: Moments to Remember, Moments Best Forgotten," *The New York Times*, November 8, 1990. https://www.nytimes.com/1990/11/08/us/the-1990-elections-the-1990-campaign-moments-to-remember-moments-best-forgotten.html

150 ¶1: Michigan Supreme Court Historical Society, "Martha Griffiths."

151 ¶1: Cohen, Alex and Wilfred U. Codrington III. "The Equal Rights Amendment Explained." The Brennan Center, January 23, 2020. https://www.brennancenter.org/our-work/research-reports/equal-rights-amendment-explained.

151 ¶2: Bellafante, Ginia. "Before Ocasio-Cortez, the Elizabeth Holtzman Effect," *The New York Times*, July 5, 2018. https://www.nytimes.com/2018/07/05/nyregion/before-ocasio-cortez-the-elizabeth-holtzman-effect.html.

153 ¶1: Bellafante, "Before Ocasio-Cortez"; "Holtzman, Elizabeth 1941–." United States House of Representatives History, Art & Archives, n.d. https://history.house.gov/People/Listing/H/HOLTZMAN,-Elizabeth-(H000752).

CHAPTER 10:
PATSY TAKEMOTO MINK

154: Lee, Ellen. "Patsy Takemoto Mink's Trailblazing Testimony Against a Supreme Court Nominee." *The Atlantic*, September 16, 2018. https://www.theatlantic.com/politics/archive/2018/09/patsy-takemoto-minks-trailblazing-testimony-against-a-supreme-court-nominee/570082.

155 ¶1: "Patsy Mink." National Park Service, n.d. https://www.nps.gov/people/patsy-mink.htm; Murphy, Michael J., ed., "Gwendolyn Mink." Oral History Transcript, March 2016.; Mertens, Richard. "Political Pioneer." *The University of Chicago Magazine*, Sept/Oct 2012. https://mag.uchicago.edu/law-policy-society/political-pioneer#; Frail, T. A. "The Injustice of Japanese Internment Camps Resonates Strongly to This Day." *Smithsonian Magazine*, January/February 2017. https://www.smithsonianmag.com/history/injustice-japanese-americans-internment-camps-resonates-strongly-180961422.

155 ¶2: *Korematsu v. United States.* Oyez. https://www.oyez.org/cases/1940-1955/323us214.

157 ¶1: Murphy, "Gwendolyn Mink"; Clinton, Hillary, and Chelsea Clinton. *The Book of Gutsy Women: Favorite Stories of Courage and Resilience*, 84. New York: Simon & Schuster, 2019.

157 ¶2: Overly, Younghee. "Patsy Mink's Legacy Lives On, but There's More to be Done. *Honolulu Civil Beat*, January 23, 2020. https://www.civilbeat.org/2020/01/patsy-minks-legacy-lives-on-but-theres-more-to-be-done; Murphy, "Gwendolyn Mink."

158 ¶1: Overly, "More to be Done"; Stewart, Alicia W. "Mother Changes the World for Daughter." Fox8 News, June 23, 2012; Murphy, "Gwendolyn Mink"; Mertens, "Political Pioneer."

158 ¶2: Lee, "Trailblazing Testimony"; Murphy, "Gwendolyn Mink."

159 ¶1: "Patsy T. Mink: Late A Representative from Hawaii: Memorial Address and Other Tributes Hon. Patsy T. Mink 1927–2002." U.S. Government Printing Office, n.d. https://www.govinfo.gov/content/pkg/CPRT-107JPRT82489/html/CPRT-107JPRT82489.htm.

159 ¶2: Clinton and Clinton, pg. 84.

159 SIDEBAR: Lili'uokalani. *Hawai'i's Story by Hawai'i's Queen.* Boston: Lee and Shepard, 1898.

159 ¶3: "Mink, Patsy Takemoto 1927–2002." United States House of Representatives History, Art & Archives, n.d. https://history.house.gov/People/detail/18329

160 ¶1: Clinton and Clinton, pg. 84.

161 ¶1: *Korematsu v. United States.*

161 ¶2: "Patsy T. Mink Sworn In as First Asian American Woman and woman of Color in Congress." History.com, March 26, 2021. https://www.history.com/this-day-in-history/patsy-mink-sworn-in-first-asian-american-woman-of-color-in-congress; Mertens, Richard. "Political Pioneer."

161 ¶3: Clinton and Clinton, pg. 84.

162 ¶1: Murphy, "Gwendolyn Mink"; Mink, Gwendolyn. "My Mother Was One of the First Women to Run for President." *Time*, June 9, 2016. https://time.com/4362066/hillary-clinton-democratic-nominee-patsy-mink.

163 ¶3: Murphy, "Gwendolyn Mink."

163 ¶4: Suk, Julie. *We the Women: The Unstoppable Mothers of the Equal Rights Amendment*, 70, 78, 112. New York: Skyhorse Publishing, 2020.

164 SIDEBAR: Lee, "Trailblazing Testimony"; Mink, "My Mother."

164 ¶1: Suk, 78.

165 ¶2: Rudin, Ken, "On This Day In 1991: House Members March to the Senate In Thomas Protest." NPR, October 8, 2010. https://www.npr.org/sections/itsallpolitics/2010/10/07/130415738/on-this-day-in-1991-female-house-members-march-to-senate-in-thomas-protest.

168 ¶2: United States House of Representatives, "Mink, Patsy."

169 ¶1: Lee, "Trailblazing Testimony."

CHAPTER 11:
BARBARA JORDAN

70: "Barbara Jordan's Life Timeline." Barbara Jordan Freedom Foundation, n.d. https://www.barbarajordanfreedomfoundation.org/barbara-jordans-life-timeline.

171 ¶2: Moss, J. Jennings. "Barbara Jordan: The Other Life." *The Advocate*, March 5, 1996. https://www.houstonlgbthistory.org/Houston80s/Houston-Advocate/Advocate-030596-BarbaraJordan.compressed.pdf.

171 ¶3: Levinson, Isaiah. "Black History Month Spotlight: Barbara Jordan," Victory Institute, February 14, 2020. https://victoryinstitute.org/black-history-month-spotlight-barbara-jordan; Moss, "Barbara Jordan."

173 ¶1: Associated Press. "Barbara Jordan Is Hospitalized," *The New York Times*, July 31, 1988. https://www.nytimes.com/1988/07/31/us/barbara-jordan-is-hospitalized.html; Moss, "Barbara Jordan."

173 ¶2: Associated Press, "Barbara Jordan Is Hospitalized."

173 ¶3: Jordan, Barbara and Shelby Hearon. *Barbara Jordan: A Self-Portrait*, 22. New York: Doubleday, 1979; Rogers, Mary Beth. *Barbara Jordan: American Hero*, 1. New York: Bantam, 2000; Russell-Cole, Kathy, Midge Wilson, and Ronald Hall. *The Color Complex: The Politics of Skin Color Among African Americans*, 39. New York: Anchor, 1992.

174 ¶2: Jordan, Barbara and Shelby Hearon. "Barbara Jordan: A Self-Portrait." *The Washington Post*, January 7, 1979. https://www.washingtonpost.com/archive/lifestyle/magazine/1979/01/07/barbara-jordan-a-self-portrait/413aa701-8a85-4c89-8781-1b02b0b8eba3; Rogers, pg. 4.

174 ¶3: Jordan and Hearon, *Barbara Jordan*, p. 62.

175 ¶1: Rogers, pg. 43; Barbara Jordan Freedom Foundation, "Life Timeline"; Broyles, William. "The Making of Barbara Jordan." *Texas Monthly*, October 1976 https://www.texasmonthly.com/news-politics/major-barbara.

175 ¶2: "Barbara C. Jordan," History.com, February 22, 2021. https://www.history.com/topics/black-history/barbara-c-jordan.

175 ¶3: Barbara Jordan Freedom Foundation, "Life Timeline."

176 SIDEBAR: Burka, Paul. "Major Barbara," *Texas Monthly*, March 1996. https://www.texasmonthly.com/news-politics/major-barbara.

176 ¶1: Burka, "Major Barbara."

178 ¶1: Barbara Jordan Freedom Foundation, "Life Timeline."

178 ¶2: Nixon Impeachment hearings, 1974; Speech by

Barbara Jordan to the House Judiciary Committee. https://www.watergate.info/1974/07-25.

179 SIDEBAR: Broyles, "The Making of Barbara Jordan."

179 ¶2: Jordan and Hearon, "Barbara Jordan: A Self-Portrait."

180 ¶1: Kelly, Kate. "The ERA Is Queer and It Always Has Been." *The Advocate*, January 27, 2021. https://www.advocate.com/commentary/2021/1/27/era-queer-and-it-always-has-been.

180 ¶2: Lardner, James and Neil Henry. "Over 40,000 ERA Backers March on Hill." *The Washington Post*, July 10, 1978. https://www.washingtonpost.com/archive/politics/1978/07/10/over-40000-era-backers-march-on-hill/880a1a29-c7ba-46f7-afd3-ade684653e63.

181 EXTRACT: Jordan, Barbara. "A Statement by Representative Barbara Jordan on May 18, 1978." Digital Public Library of America. https://dp.la/primary-source-sets/the-equal-rights-amendment/sources/1206.

181: ¶1: Suk, Julie. *We the Women: The Unstoppable Mothers of the Equal Rights Amendment*, 119. New York: Skyhorse Publishing, 2020.

182 ¶1: Broyles, "The Making of Barbara Jordan."

184 ¶1: Hines, Cragg. "A Voice for Justice Dies; Barbara Jordan Lived as a Pioneer and Prophet." *Houston Chronicle*, January 18, 1996.

184 ¶2: "Barbara Jordan Funeral." Video recording. 1:40:49. C-SPAN. January 20, 1996. https://www.c-span.org/video/?69467-1/barbara-jordan-funeral.

185 ¶2: Channing, Cornelia. "What's Fact and What's Fiction in Mrs. America." Slate, April 15, 2020. https://slate.com/culture/2020/04/mrs-america-accuracy-fact-fiction-fx-hulu-miniseries.html.

185 ¶3: Beckwith, Ryan Teague. "What You Should Know About Phyllis Schlafly." *Time*, September 6, 2016. https://time.com/4480208/phyllis-schlafly-election-history.

185 ¶4: Iber, Patrick. "How the GOP Became the Party of Resentment." *The New Republic*, August 11, 2020. https://newrepublic.com/article/158680/republican-party-resentment-reaganland-rick-perlstein-book-review.

186 ¶1: Elliott, Justin. "The Hypocrisy of Phyllis Schlafly." Salon, April 1, 2011. https://www.salon.com/2011/04/01/phyllis_schlafly_child_care.

186 ¶2: Kelly, Kate and Jamia Wilson. "Foot Soldiers of the Patriarchy." Ordinary Equality. Podcast audio. February 18, 2020. https://podcasts.apple.com/us/podcast/foot-soldiers-of-the-patriarchy/id1492330633?i=1000465931371.

187 ¶3: Lardner and Henry, "Over 40,000 ERA Backers"; Balmer, Randal. "Phyllis Schlafly: The Antifeminist Who Wanted a Job in the Reagan Administration." *Los Angeles Times*, September 8, 2016. https://www.latimes.com/opinion/op-ed/la-oe-balmer-phyllis-schlafly-reagan-appointments-20160908-snap-story.html.

CHAPTER 12: PAT SPEARMAN

189 ¶3: Kelly, Kate. "First Congressional Hearing on the ERA in 36 Years." Equality Now, May 2, 2019. https://www.equalitynow.org/era_hearing_april2019.

191 ¶1: "Herstory," Spearman4Nevada, n.d. https://spearman4nevada.com/herstory.

191 ¶2: "Herstory."

194 ¶1: "Herstory"; Suk, Julie. *We the Women: The Unstoppable Mothers of the Equal Rights Amendment*, 129. New York: Skyhorse Publishing, 2020.

194 ¶2: Sebelius, Steve. "Champion for Equality." *Las Vegas Review-Journal*, February 21, 2020. https://www.reviewjournal.com/news/politics-and-government/nevada/for-pat-spearman-the-fight-for-equality-is-the-fight-of-her-life-1961701/.

195 ¶1: Sebelius, "Champion"; Brown, Soni. "How Pat Spearman Went from the Pulpit to the Polls." *The Nevada Independent*, May 20, 2018. https://thenevadaindependent.com/article/how-pat-spearman-went-from-the-pulpit-to-the-polls.

195 ¶2: Brown, "Pulpit to Polls"; Sebelius, "Champion."

197 SIDEBAR: Brown, "Pulpit to Polls."

198 SIDEBAR: Dolores Huerta on Why We Need the Equal Rights Amendment. Facebook. Feminist Majority Foundation, 2021. https://www.facebook.com/watch/?v=1049611868864583.

198 ¶1: Rodriguez, Barbara. "How a New Generation of Lawmakers Led by Black Women Revived the Equal Rights Amendment." The 19th, March 15, 2021. https://19thnews.org/2021/03/black-women-era-revival.

199 ¶1: Spearman, Pat. Testimony, Senate Committee on Legislative Operations and Elections. February 2, 2017.

200 SIDEBAR: MacCammon, Sarah. "For These Women, the Equal Rights Amendment Has Been a Decades-Long Battle." NPR, January 15, 2020. https://www.npr.org/2020/01/15/796645936/for-these-women-the-equal-rights-amendment-has-been-a-decades-long-battle.

200 ¶1: Rodriguez, "New Generation."

201 ¶1: Rodriguez, "New Generation."

201 ¶3: Olivo, Antonio. "Danica Roem of Virginia to Be First Openly Transgender Person Elected, Seated in a U.S. Statehouse." *The Washington Post*, November 8, 2017. https://www.washingtonpost.com/local/virginia-politics/danica-roem-will-be-vas-first-openly-transgender-elected-official-after-unseating-conservative-robert-g-marshall-in-house-race/2017/11/07/d534bdde-c0af-11e7-959c-fe2b598d8c00_story.html.

201 ¶4: Cheslow, Daniella. "Meet the Virginia Lawmaker Who Got the Equal Rights Amendment Tattooed on Her Arm." WAMU.org, January 28, 2020. https://wamu.org/story/20/01/28/meet-the-virginia-lawmaker-who-got-the-equal-rights-amendment-tattooed-on-her-arm.

CONCLUSION: FUTURE FRAMERS

205 ¶1: Stanton, Elizabeth Cady, Susan B. Anthony, and Matilda Joslyn Gage. *History of Woman Suffrage*, vol. 1 (1881) 31.

208 ¶1: Rodriguez, Barbara. "How a New Generation of Lawmakers Led by Black Women Revived the Equal Rights Amendment." The 19th, March 15, 2021. https://19thnews.org/2021/03/black-women-era-revival.

THERE WILL NEVER BE A NEW WORLD ORDER UNTIL WOMEN ARE A PART OF IT. -Alice Paul

#RADICALSELFRESPECT

Let it be known: I did not fall from grace. I leapt to freedom. -Ansel Elkins

ABOUT THE AUTHOR

Kate Kelly is a feminist, activist, and human rights lawyer. She holds a JD degree from American University Washington College of Law, the only law school in the country founded by and for women (and Alice Paul's alma mater). She's a nationally known advocate for the ratification of the Equal Rights Amendment and host and creator of the podcast Ordinary Equality. Kate lives in Washington, DC, with her partner, Jamie Manson. You can follow her on Twitter at @kate_kelly_esq. To learn more about the Equal Rights Amendment and for an up-to-date list of news and articles about its current progress, visit www.ordinaryequality.com!

RAISE HELL, KID.

HERE IS THE WORLD. BEAUTIFUL AND TERRIBLE THINGS WILL HAPPEN.

Moshi the Wondercat

THIS IS THE SEASON SHE WILL MAKE BEAUTIFUL THINGS. NOT PERFECT THINGS.

BUT HONEST THINGS THAT SPEAK TO WHO SHE IS

AND WHO SHE IS CALLED TO BE.

—Morgan Harper Nichols

SMALLANDMIGHTY

DO NOT BE AFRAID.

ABOUT THE ARTIST

Nicole LaRue is a graphic designer, illustrator, and author. She believes every person, no matter their age or status, can help create positive social change. Called upon at the eleventh hour to create the official logo for the 2017 Women's March on Washington, Nicole is no stranger to mighty work. Her clients include Chronicle Books, Abrams Books, Oxford University Press, Compendium, Inc., Madison Park Greetings, Johnson & Johnson, Chatbooks, Tiny Prints, DC Shoes, Spumoni Studio, American Eagle, and more. See her work at www.smallmadegoods.com. Nicole resides in Salt Lake City, Utah.